Living Beneath the Radar

A Nine-Year Journey Around the World

"He who travels far will often see things far removed from what he believes was truth. When he talks about it in the fields at home, he is often accused of lying, for the obdurate people will not believe what they do not see and distinctly feel. Inexperience, I believe, will give little credence to my song." (Quote by Hermann Hesse)

I0200937

Cover Pictures

Author with Mt. Everest in Background
Hanging from a bridge on Everest Trek
Author in 1970 two weeks before leaving

Copyright 2012 Jeffrey R. Crimmel

Cover Design for 2nd Edition

Michelle Radomski

One Voice Publishing Solutions

Michelle@onevoicepublishingsolutions.co

ISBN-13: 978-0985223236

DEDICATION

This book is dedicated to the world travelers who took a chance and got off the cruise ship and ventured into the neighborhoods to see the people and customs of those countries. Also to the travelers who visit countries on their own and find out that the world is made up of many different customs and religions which are different than theirs and are not threatened by those differences. Travel to me is the best possible education available to us in the world today and for those of you who decide to take this course in higher learning, I salute you.

Forward

By Scott Anderson

Most of us that lived through the 1970s remember it as a decade of change and experimentation – out with the old and in with the new and excitingly different. Who of us doesn't remember at least trying on a pair of bellbottom pants and platform shoes, and a night of disco dancing to go along with them? It was a decade in which, for a brief time, Pet rocks became the favorite pet, Saturday Night Fever had nothing to do with medicine, jogging became the favorite personal sport, and the first examples of what would become one of our most important electronic sidekicks – the personal computer. Then there were our favorite television programs – The Waltons, Starsky and Hutch, Charlie's Angels, and The Muppets.

There was the publication of the Pentagon Papers, the awakening of OPEC and the Middle East oil embargo, the end of the Vietnam War, and the break-in at the Watergate office building that ultimately led to the only resignation of a US President – Richard Nixon. And let's not forget the US Bicentennial celebration in 1976.

Most of us remember these things and more because we experienced them firsthand. But Jeff Crimmel did not. Jeff never owned a Pet Rock, nor was he familiar with those popular TV shows, All in the Family or Happy Days. He did not listen to disco, nor I am told, did he ever wear bellbottom pants, and, being a tall man himself, he never tried on a pair of platform shoes.

But what Jeff Crimmel did do during the 1970s was something extraordinary – he left behind what he knew, growing up in southern California in the 50s and 60s, and set out on a nine-year journey to places that most of the rest of us could only dream about. I remember myself, at times during the 1970s thinking about exotic places that I had learned about in college. Places like Australia, India, Afghanistan, Iran, Turkey and Greece. While I was dreaming about these places, Jeff Crimmel was living and traveling there. Alternately a clothes and jewelry merchant from the Far East to Europe, a surfer in Goa, India, a potential fomenter of religious revolution in the home of the Taliban, Jeff Crimmel lived the life of a traveling hippie, a seeker of Eastern knowledge, a homesteader in the outback of Australia. He saw sights that we today will never be able to see, including ancient ways of life – unchanged in centuries – in Heart and Kabul, Afghanistan.

Read this book if you will. You will come away with a very different perspective on life during the 70s. You will laugh and you will learn. Most of all, you will get to share in the experiences of a young man, out in the world in search of adventure and understanding of other cultures, and Living Beneath the Radar. You will not be disappointed.

Scott Anderson

February 2010

Books by Author

Non Fiction

Learning to Love the Peso; How to Move to Mexico and Why

Centavo; A Dog from Mexico

The 60's, If You Remember it You didn't Live It.

Fiction

Brain Bleed

Ian's Revenge

Nab Yoga

The Hemp Papers

Contents

This is the second edition of Living Beneath the Radar.

ACKNOWLEDGMENTS

I would like to thank the people of the world during the 70'a for giving me an education that one can only obtain by making this journey. I had some close calls at times and always felt I had a guardian angel watching over me. Some of the situation were so dire that I couldn't even put them into the book.

I now have two grown daughters who have grown up as independent females and are strong in who they are. I let them grown on their own and they found their way all by themselves. Their mother, Pavitra, was also a strong influence on their lives and I know they appreciate her and still think of her all the time.

Lastly I want to encourage anyone thinking about travel and seeing another culture. My hope is you can do so with an open mind and take from your experience what you need in future decisions. We are a world population made up of many religions, languages, and customs and there is not one way to make this work. My hope is my story can be an inspiration for you.

Jeffrey Ray Crimmel

Chapter 1
Choices in Life

How each of us got to where we are in our life is a mystery many ask. When I retired, I signed up for Facebook along with my high school and college alumni web page. I wanted to find out which of my classmates I outlived.

When I did this and started to look at the pictures of those with whom I shared the sacred halls of learning 45 years ago, I was totally amazed as to how they all aged. Most had gained weight as I had and now were going through the golden years of their lives, many still living near San Diego where they grew up.

Looking back at how I got to where I am in life came about because of a single choice I made in 1971. Had I not made this decision I too may be living in the San Diego area having never ventured out into the world to see what was going on. The direction I took changed my life dramatically. The journey had begun.

Chapter 2
The Early Years

High School in my town was mostly shared with others whom I grew up with in elementary and Junior High. During those years, bonds were made and broken. Life long friendships were developed and lost and many of us never meet each other again except for those who return to reunions because high school became the best part of their lives.

Of all the students I remember attending my high school, Raquel Welch seemed to be the only one who strived to be in the limelight and live above the radar.

My hometown, La Jolla, is exactly what the word translates from in Spanish. The Jewel. It is a beautiful coastal southern California community made up of many wealthy families. They posted their importance in the local newspaper (La Jolla Light) with photos showing how big their party became over the weekend. The list of who attended always added to the shallow report of the gathering. Little substance emerged from the community rag.

Residents are mostly conservative, rich and Republican. They still hold onto the trickle down theory of "This is mine and if there are any crumbs left you can have them." Their children tend to return to town after they go off to have their college experience, because the parents have built a business or professional niche for them to follow in their footsteps. Doctors, lawyers, real estate brokers and hardware shop owners to name just a few.

I knew six people of color with whom I went to classes with from elementary through high school. Of the six I remember, one was a star track and football player named Butch. Another black student from La Jolla became a star basketball player for a team my younger brother played on. His name was Charlie and I got to play on the same Little League baseball team with him. We won the championship that year. Charlie was the winning pitcher.

The 1964 basketball team, which Charlie led, went undefeated for the season but lost the city championship game in a blowout. Charlie went on to college in Arizona on a basketball scholarship. I heard he did not stay and finish due to the pressures of his being gay in an era that did not support such a lifestyle.

The third black student I remember was a girl whom I knew in elementary school as well as high school. Jeanne won the vote of the student body as a cheerleader in a white, sliced bread school with the help of the "cool crowd" who campaigned for her. That was one of the most amazing accomplishments I witnessed at La Jolla High.

The reason I have mentioned the ethnic color makeup of La Jolla, while I was growing up, is to show my limited exposure to black or brown America. In seven short years, I would be traveling in a world primarily made up of cultures with every color other than white. I would forever be impacted by such a world discovery.

Most parents do things for their children to prepare them for what they know to be the lifestyle best suited for them. My mother was no exception. She spent years trying to get me to grasp the benefits of the La Jolla

Country Club lifestyle, which she became a part of when my parents were married.

Ballroom dance classes became a big part of the introduction to social life. It was an event I enjoyed because I could move my feet. Of all the fox trots and waltzes, the dance, in which I won with the same partner two years running is best remembered. This number would never make the "So You Think You Can Dance" TV show. It was performed at the end of the six-week lesson session. The ballroom school held a party to show the attending parents how their money was spent in their attempt to get the kids ready for the La Jolla society lifestyle.

The performance started off with a grapefruit placed between the foreheads of the dancers. The fruit needed to remain between the pair until a winner, through the process of elimination, was declared. In other words, 'the last grapefruit standing.'

My partner, being my height and not easily embarrassed, became a perfect match. Our bodies attempted to keep the fruit from dropping by squeezing tightly together. As the yellow sphere slipped from our foreheads down towards our necks and upper torso regions, the intense pressure continued. The fruit never made it below the belt line. If such an event occurred the teacher would have stopped the music and declared the remaining dancers all winners before the viewing parents could leap up and scream, "This has gone too far." Oh well, so much for La Jolla society life.

Chapter 3
Europe 1963

I left La Jolla in the summer of 1963 on a gifted tour of Europe my mother gave me after graduation. Her intent seemed to center around her desire to separate me from surfing, which by now became a big part of my life. The sport held no place in La Jolla society.

At the time I held a job at a burger joint selling five burgers for a dollar. If you only wanted one burger the cost was nineteen cents each. Nobody stopped to do the math and most people paid the dollar for the package of five. The Swede, who owned the fast food restaurant, must have known Americans were not good with numbers.

Not only did I have a job, I was only two blocks away from good surfing in Pacific Beach. Why would I want to leave such a utopian lifestyle for a chance to broaden my world perspective? I bet there are no five hamburgers for a dollar eating establishments in Europe. I really did not want to go but somehow I was persuaded. The possibility of experiencing something new and have my first flight in a 707, the big plane in 1963, changed my mind.

My mother's other plan for sending me to Europe was to educate me in European cultures, learn a language and come back ready to fit into the life she planned for me. I was eighteen. The drinking age in Europe was sixteen. We were going to be left in Salzburg, Austria learning German for three weeks without escorts. What was she thinking?

The tour of Europe was a real awakening for me. I loved the place the moment I got off the plane. People speaking different languages and wearing different clothing styles was like being in a foreign country. Guess what? I was.

The main part of the tour placed students either in Salzburg, learning German, or Paris for those who wanted to learn French. I chose Salzburg because all the cute girls on the tour were going to Salzburg. Remember, I am eighteen at the time and hormones won out over good decisions every time.

After the first week of summer school, my roommate and I attended only two of the German classes. The freedom of being left alone with out adult supervision was more than we could handle. The nightlife in Salzburg goes until 2 am. Many nights, during the three-week German learning period, we entered our room through the bathroom window. (I believe the Beatles wrote a song about entering through the bathroom window.) The front door was locked at 10 pm and the Dormer (German for window) remained our only possible avenue back to our beds. Learning German for the summer became a lost cause. Becoming a connoisseur of the many different beers made in Austria turned out to be a big part of my pre-college education.

I ended up living in Salzburg for a year. A family by the name of Mastnak took me in as an exchange student. There was something about going where and when I wanted which needed further exploration. Surfing did take a backstage to the experiences of living in a European city. I was learning how to balance my life and give it direction as I entered into adulthood. I needed to sow a few wild oats. Having fun and living in a different culture became my post La Jolla High School project for the decision I made six years later. My younger brother, Randy, later told me the lifestyle I lived, while in Europe destroyed any chance for him and my other two siblings from having the same opportunity of going to Europe after they graduated from high school. I think the attempt by my mother to make her children ready for La Jolla society would have to take another venue. The adventures in Europe helped me appreciate my position as the oldest of the children.

Chapter 4
UCSB 1964-1969

The school, which I received acceptance to the year before I went to Europe, was the University of California at Santa Barbara. Playboy magazine listed it in the top ten party colleges in the nation. The dorms overlooked the ocean and perfect waves were breaking within a five-minute walk down the cliff path to the beach. People in the dorms kept surfboards in the corner of their rooms, right next to the desk and books. When the waves were big, the books would wait. If the winter brought good surf, grade point averages dropped. It was not a choice of which college to attend when you went to UCSB. A surfing lifestyle with education thrown in on the side was the UCSB decision for many.

There were two people I remember who went to UCSB, during the time I attended, who qualified as "living above the radar." One was a guitar player who later went on to play with The Doors. A friend later told me his name was Robbie Krieger.

Kirk Douglas's kid also attended UCSB. That is how Michael Douglas was referred to from 1964 to 1968. We all knew who Kirk Douglas was but no one knew Michael Douglas. I never did meet him and I now wish I enrolled in some acting classes then.

College represented the American transition from youth to adulthood. I lived in Santa Barbara from 1964 to 1969. Issues like Vietnam, Flower Power, Reagan as Governor, Johnson as president, and which side to choose, forced many of us to grow up quickly or stayed stoned until the 70's. I did a little of both. Somehow I graduated in February of 1969, changing my major from Economics to Geography during my senior year. I could do math with ease but my interest in foreign countries became much more of a focus than becoming an accountant. I am sure the study of Geography influenced my decision to travel the world from 1970 to 1979.

Upon graduation I chose not to pursue a lifetime occupation. I made a decision not to follow the path others before me took. Working from age twenty-five to sixty, retire, travel, play golf and relocate to Arizona or Florida did not fit as a lifestyle for me. Del Webb built communities to accommodate those individuals and I wanted no part of it.

One thing I did know: I was fortunate to be in my position at age twenty-two. I did not want to blow it. I held a 1Y military classification after the army spent two and a half years trying to mold me into becoming a second lieutenant in the college R.O.T.C. program. My back was injured in my junior year while moving a barbell weight. The only way the military might use me depended upon the United States declaring war in Vietnam. That never happened. The conflict remained a police action. Many men died while policing Vietnam.

Chapter 5
The Army Draft

My process of going through the army physical exam and draft induction became an experience Arlo Guthrie might have written a song about. It was a chaotic time and unlike Alice's Restaurant, you could not get anything you wanted. If the government drew your number you needed to go to an induction center for a complete exam. If you passed the physical you were to be drafted into the Army and shipped off to Vietnam.

I lived in Santa Barbara at the time and I needed to go to the downtown Los Angeles induction center. I received a letter saying two buses, dispatched by the US Army, would pick me up along with forty young men, ages eighteen to twenty-five years old, from a certain location at 7:00 a.m. in Santa Barbara.

Arriving around 6:30 I noticed about twenty-five young men my age, serious and ready to be drafted and serve their country. They already wore military haircuts and all that remained was the physical exam. Eight men, like myself, held letters from doctors describing some type of physical handicap prohibiting us from serving in the armed forces. The last group of seven men dressed like they just walked off the streets of Haight-Ashbury in San Francisco.

This last group I will call the "Santa Barbara Seven." They wore flowers in their hair, tie-dye shirts, and bell-bottom pants. A few carried tambourines and musical instruments with them. They were prepared to make this experience a memorable one. I recognized one of them as a UCSB student from a few years before. Several years had passed since I last saw him. It appeared the members of the group had tuned in, turned on and dropped out following Timothy Leary's directions on how to fight the establishment.

The wait for the busses took a while. Separate groups among the forty men formed. Each of us seemed to gravitate to one another based on haircuts and types of clothing worn. The Santa Barbara Seven became a group by themselves. They started playing some music as we waited and soon the familiar smell of that special plant from Mexico filled the air. A joint made its' way through the waiting crowd with an open invitation for anyone to participate. I have never run for political office and I never will. Unlike Bill Clinton, I did inhale.

The busses pulled up twenty minutes later. The first bus filled with those young men on a mission to join the army, and serve their country. The second bus included the eight of us carrying medical papers or letters from our doctors. The Santa Barbara Seven also joined us on the second bus. They were fairly stoned by now and it was only 7:30 am.

The two-hour drive to the Los Angeles induction center from Santa Barbara seemed to take an eternity. During the trip the Santa Barbara Seven continued the music in the back of the bus. Accompanying the music came the continuous smell of thick Mary Jane smoke. It eventually reached the front of the bus and the bus driver. Second-hand smoke can be just as powerful as first-hand smoke when it comes to Marijuana and I am sure the driver started feeling the effects. He yelled at the seven in the rear of the bus.

"Put out those joints or I'll pull over and throw you all off the bus."

If the same situation happened today the outcome would be different. One of the young men would have held out a piece of paper for the bus driver to see and say, "I have a doctor's prescription so I'm legal."

*****

An hour later the bus pulled up to the induction center. As I gazed out the window of the bus all I could see was a crowd of protesters, filling the sidewalk. Many carried signs expressing their feelings about the Vietnam War. The messages protested against the government sending off young men to be killed in an unjust foreign war. It looked like a scene from Forrest Gump except this time I found myself written into the script, and life was not like a box of chocolates.

The military draft in our country affected thousands of young men across our country. I remembered in 1964 when I returned to California from Europe. I took the bus across the country because I wanted to see what our United States looked like up close and personal. The bus pulled into countless small towns in the mid-west and at every stop young men, eighteen years and older, were saying good-bye to their girlfriends and families. They were off to the boot camps in different parts of the country. The U.S. was gearing up for the Vietnam conflict. Thousands of these young men did not return from Vietnam and those who did were not given the welcome they thought they deserved. I never supported the war but I feel the country let the returning forces down by not giving them the support they needed so they could re-adjust to civilian life.

All of a sudden the bus door opened and a huge army drill sergeant, probably six feet four inches tall and 275 pounds of prime army conditioning, walked onto the bus and began barking out orders.

"I want each one of you to stand up and file out of this bus keeping your eyes straight ahead as you enter the building. You will not turn your head to either side. Pay no attention to these protesters who are trying to stop you from serving your country. Is that understood?"

We all stood up and began filing out of the bus and into the building. I can still remember the young women protesters as they approached us shouting,

"They don't own you. You do not need to do this. You are being used to fight a war killing women and children."

Fortunately, the walk from the bus to the induction center took only twenty steps. I did my best to keep my head facing forward therefore not attracting the wrath of the huge army sergeant who gave us orders not to look in any direction other than straight forward. The year 1967 became a time when many young men made a choice and this decision would change their lives forever.

As I entered the recruiting center the movie I found myself observing the play as it just kept unfolding. A young man, with flaming red hair and size almost equal to the sergeant who gave us those first instructions on the bus, started to argue with a smaller army corporal. The red head was yelling,

"You can't tell me what to do. I am not in the army and you can't make me do anything."

Sometimes size makes people do stupid things. This guy may have possessed the size to order people around but he used it in the wrong place. He became outnumbered quickly and the yelling drew the attention of my favorite sergeant. He came over to confront the unwilling citizen. When the sergeant arrived, the face of the 'almost as big' red head changed. His expression said, shit, I think I just blew it.

The sergeant asked the young man to hand him his induction papers. The young man reluctantly gave them to the sergeant. He just stood there trying to put up a front for all of us still standing in line and watching this confrontation play out in the corner of our eyes. Our heads were still facing forward. The sergeant said to the young man,

"Ok, you're free to go. Your papers will be handed in and stamped as refusing to follow directions. You will be notified in the mail as to what the U.S government will do with you."

I may never again witness a young man, as large this guy, lose six inches of height and one hundred pounds of weight as he shrunk down and into the body of a small teenager. He started to beg the sergeant to give him back his papers and allow him to go through the physical examination. He knew he screwed with the wrong man and may have made a bad choice. My line kept moving forward. The last time I observed the humbled red head, he was being escorted out of the building and into the crowd of protesters on the street. His life just took a turn and he now needed to live with it.

I don'tt remember too much of the physical exam. The testing consisted mostly of young men bending over and spreading their cheeks, coughing and being herded into the next room. At the end of the physical exam a corporal came up to our group and said,

"If anyone possesses medical or psychological paperwork from a doctor, go up to the third floor and wait until you're called."

I knew my winning ticket was about to be drawn. I possessed a medical paper and I continued to pass "Go" and collect $200.

The third floor became another chapter in this on-going movie. As I sat on a bench, waiting my turn to see the doctor, I noticed another young man on a bench all by himself. He wore long, black, oily hair and dressed in a black leather jacket, black leather pants, and a black shirt, which made his pale white skin stand out like a neon sign. Johnnie Cash comes to mind when describing the young man and this guy look like he just emerged from "The Ring of Fire." He rocked back and forth holding his arms across his body. An aura surrounded him with a message attached to it saying,

'Stay away from me! I took a whole lot of pills this morning and I am not going to go into the army. I want them to think I am crazy.'

No one went near him and I never saw him again.

Many young men did many different things to stop from being drafted and go into the army. Each held their reasons for joining or not wanting to be a part of the army. The pressures on young men during the Vietnam conflict were tremendous. There are those who are suited for military life and those who are not. The U.S. government, with the draft policy, took everyone. Those men not suited for military life experienced a miserable time. If they were fortunate enough to have received an education they may have found a position doing military office work. The others were put into the field and given a gun.

I held a letter from a doctor. I did not need to choose any of the other options many young men, who were not military material, made.

I looked around the room again and noticed an army corporal making his rounds with other young men like myself. He proceeded to grab papers out of the hands of each person who waited to be seen by a doctor. He read the letters and made some negative comment. He tried to get a rise out of each young man. The actions of the corporal seemed to be his job. He allowed no one to escape the torment. He soon made his way to me, grabbed the papers out of my hands and yelled,

"What's the matter with you?"

He read the papers and looked down at me with a look of disgust. He must have practiced the expression each day in front of a mirror before he went to work.

"It says here you have a bad back."

"Yes," I answered.

"Can you fuck?" he shot back.

The eyes of all the other young men in the room turned on me. At the age of twenty-two, sex seemed to be everything a male stood for. My answer would determine my manhood in their eyes.

"Yes," I answered. A sigh of relief seemed to come from the other observers in the room.

"Well, if you can fuck you can fight," he fired back. Slamming the papers on the bench next to me, he moved on to the next victim.

Had I been quick, brave or stupid enough I would have answered,

"You mean when we are in Vietnam all we are going to do is fuck and fight?"

Silence remained the best answer in many situations and I chose not to respond to this one.

The third-floor talk with the doctor lasted about thirty minutes. After many questions, he brought out a stamp and classified me as 1Y. 1Y is a free pass to live through the Vietnam conflict and not become target practice for the Viet Cong thousands of miles away.

I made my way to the exit of the induction center and out the front door. I looked to my left as I walked onto the sidewalk. No army soldier stood at the door telling me to only look forward. As I viewed the crowd of protestors I was amazed but not completely surprised by whom I saw. Among the crowd stood the 'Santa Barbara Seven'. They were smoking joints and carrying signs with the rest of the American youth I saw while getting off the bus. The seven men never made it into the induction center. They must have stepped off the bus and turned right. Each one made a decision and never looked back. They were not army material. Like the red-headed young man who left the building without taking the physical, these men also were about to have their lives change forever. I often wonder how many of them live in Canada today.

Chapter 6
The Post College Year

My preparation to leave the United States started with my having to work, saving money and deciding where to go. I began to drive a yellow cab in Santa Barbara along with four other UCSB college graduates. We all reached a point in our lives asking ourselves,

"What do I do now?"

Driving a taxi became an insightful job. I soon found out both the rich and the poor take cabs.

The rich included one character I named Charles. He lived off a trust fund his wealthy family set up for him. He was in his thirties and already an alcoholic. He no longer could drive because of his many D.U.I.s. He owned a car but it remained parked. An Excalibur, is an English made vehicle. It looks like a Jaguar only stretched out. The seat covers were real zebra skin and the car stood out in any parking lot as a vehicle viewed by any car guy. Even Click and Clack, the Tappet Brothers, would have been impressed.

Being an alcoholic, Charles possessed an ulcer problem. The many years of drinking Scotch took a toll on his body. He now drank the same drink with a splash of milk to help line his stomach, or so he thought. He would start his day around 10 am by calling a cab. When he hired a taxi he would keep the meter running. A driver knew if he happened to be the one receiving the call to pick up Charles, his days' earnings would be high.

The few times, in which I drove Charles around town, we usually went from one saloon to another. I would play pool and watched him and others drink at the bar. Charles did not seem to be liked at the watering holes he attended. He could be loud and obnoxious. His money allowed him to do what he wanted but alcohol limited his freedom to live a fulfilling life.

The last time I ran into Charles happened near the Santa Barbara harbor where he kept his boat. One of the Yellow Cab drivers, who could put up with being around Charles for more than half an hour, came up with a compatible idea for both parties. He told Charles he could save money if he hired him as his personal driver. He would drive Charles around in his own car, the Excalibur, and have Charles pay him a salary, which would be less than his Yellow Cab bill. This clever driver would also make more as Charles's companion than as a Yellow Cab driver. The driver needed this better paying job because his wife expected twins within the month. Charles needed a friend and companion to get him safely from bar to bar. I hope their agreement lasted for a few years before Charles's liver gave out.

The poorest person I met while driving in Santa Barbara was a partially blind woman in her sixties named Mary. I remember her name because she became the most dreaded call any of the drivers would get. Excuses would fly when her address came out to the drivers.

"Oh, I just got a pickup fare off the street and I cannot get Mary."

"I think my cab needs more gas so I better fill it up."

Mary, a neglected elderly person, lived by herself in a poor part of Santa Barbara. She always took a cab to go shopping. She needed to travel to distant grocery stores because she was blackballed from all the stores near her. Her crime? She was a shoplifter. Not just a shoplifter… she was a sixty-year-old, blind shoplifter.

What she did amounted to petty theft. She walked around the store aisles and put items into her personal shopping cart, which remained always by her side. She would bury store items under dirty clothes in the cart. The clothes smelled so bad, cab drivers would carry air spray cans to clean out the stench after they brought her home.

Mary would pay for a few items she placed on top of the dirty clothes and usually get out of the store with all the other products hidden in her cart. She would create a loud fuss if anyone, other than herself, touched her cart. None of the store employees wanted to go through Mary's dirty clothing. Eventually, stores would grow tired of the obvious stealing and blind Mary would no longer be allowed to come into their establishment.

At the time I started driving for Yellow Cab in 1969, Mary needed to travel to a store eight miles away from her home. It must have taken years for Mary to be banned from shopping at all the stores within the previous seven-mile radius. Her life lacked love and caring. She seemed to have no family watching out for her and little income to live on.

Both rich and poor make choices, which direct them through life. Having money or not does not make one necessarily happy. Money is not the secret of happiness.

I have just given the reader two stories. One individual possessed money and the other did not. Both lives had limitations and appeared to be unhappy. The good decisions we make guide us towards happiness. No pressure. Happy or not we can all hire a cab.

Chapter 7
July 2009

The date today in which I am writing is July 20, 2009, and the coverage of the Lunar Landing in 1969 is filling the television networks. I find it interesting writing about my cab driving days during this 40-year remembrance. This, along with the death of John F. Kennedy, became one of those "Where were you and what were you doing" moments.

My cab-driving shift in 1969 was 11 am to 8 pm. As the evening approached America became glued to their TV sets. Each house where I stopped, either to drop off or pick up fares, watched the tube and the coverage of the landing. The moment the first man walked on the moon was the same moment I dropped off a fare at his house. He invited me in and I saw the magical moment with a family I never met. This event was one of those special ones bringing people in this country together, no matter what differences they may have. In the 60's there were many issues separating people but tonight they all came together to celebrate something special.

Chapter 8
Uncle Walter

Another big event happened several days earlier while writing this book. The passing of Walter Cronkite happened in July of 2009. As a newsman, he brought many of us, who lived during the 60's and 70's, coverage of Vietnam, the assassination of the Kennedys and Martin Luther King, the downfall of Nixon, and the landing on the moon. During one of the many interviews Uncle Walter gave to the media, I found out Mr. Cronkite came from a family of dentists. His answer to the question of why he did not follow in their footsteps and become a dentist was,

"I felt I would rather look into a horse's mouth instead of a human's mouth to find the truth."

Many sons and daughters, with parents doing dentistry as a career, did not go into this field for various reasons. I am one of them. As a child growing up, I spent time looking at my father's dentist book with the black and white photos of the different problems a dentist might confront.

I heard the human mouth is worse, compared to an animal's mouth, in the area of health. The pictures were proof. I am sure Uncle Walter saw similar photos of the diseased human mouth when he grew up. He made a choice as I did. No way! He became an icon journalist living above the radar. I traveled and eventually became a teacher living below the radar. We all miss you, Uncle Walter.

Chapter 9
I'm Out of Here

Leaving the U.S. was my plan since my year abroad in Salzburg, Austria. I fell in love with the difference Europe provided me. Besides being much older than America, Europe included a cultural history and a much more accepting quality regarding its people and their individual uniqueness. These attributes are harder to find in America.

America is isolated from the world. We live on a big island with minimum contact with our neighbors. A European learns three or four languages in school and they learn to speak them fluently. It is a necessity. One can drive in Europe for several hours and be in another country with a different language and culture.

Americans may learn one other language while in school because it is a requirement for graduation in most colleges. In contrast, they usually do not learn to speak them well. One reason for the lack of language skills relates to the American traveler. When Americans travel they expect other citizens in foreign countries to speak English. They usually do. English has replaced French as the international language a person learns when traveling the world. Do not mention this fact to a Frenchman.

While writing this book I lived in Flagstaff, AZ. When I moved there in 2000 I became surrounded with Spanish, Navajo and Hopi students. I never lived in a town containing such a large Native American population. At first, I became intimidated while shopping at Wal-Mart on Saturdays. If you want to see what it feels like to become an instant minority in Flagstaff, go to this store on a Saturday. Many families come into town from the reservation to stock up on the items sold at rock bottom prices. Families also take in a movie, which seems to be a favorite pastime, while in town. Many attempt to be a part of the white culture while still holding onto their language, beliefs, and customs. Good for them.

After being in Flagstaff for nine years I have become much more at ease. I do not notice the large population of Native Americans or Mexicans at the stores or at the movies. I just see people. They have the same concerns and desires as the white majority but they approach the white culture with caution. This concern is base on how they were treated over the years. If you are a good Billy Gonna (White Man) and you treat Native Americans with respect, they treat you with respect. Sounds like a good code to live by.

*****

I saved several thousand dollars by the summer of 1970. I worked in Lake Tahoe at Heavenly Valley ski resort, Harrah's' Club and the Long Beach Yacht Club in Southern California. My schoolmate from UCSB, Steve Rewick, just finished a master's degree at San Jose State College. He also wanted to leave the country for a while before settling down into a life occupation. He came from a wealthy family in the Chicago area and the pressures on him to start earning money and start a career probably were intense.

I flew up to the Bay Area and stayed with Steve for a few days while he finished packing up his VW van. We prepared to drive to his parent's house outside of Chicago, store what belongings we did not need to take with us to Europe and drive to New York. Both of us purchased a $99 Icelandic Airways one-way flight out of New York. Our excitement level increase as our flight date approached. This would be my second trans-America road trip. The first one happened on my return to the U.S. after living in Salzburg for a year.

Our trip across the country took us to the beautiful state of Colorado, a part of the America I never visited before. Estes Park remains today as one town I will never forget. We approached the mountain town by crossing over an eleven thousand foot pass. We could see the small community from the summit. It sat, tucked into a forest filled valley and maintained its' frontier beauty with many quaint shops and restaurants catering to the tourist trade.

We dropped by the Lang Ski Boot Company in Colorado to replace a set of their boots I purchased the year before. Ski boot companies experimented with foam and other materials in the 70's and my blue foam custom fit boots became one of those early failed attempts.

We arrived at Steve's parent's house several days later after driving through the cornfields of the heartland. I wish the Field of Dreams ballpark and all the players of past seasons were playing. We would have dropped in for a game or two. This part of the world is very boring. I now understand why fuel futurists are trying to turn the heartland into the Saudi Arabia of corn. There may be a lot of corn in America but I still want a Prius.

The week with the parents held plenty of events to pass the time. Tennis, visiting family friends at night and a trip to the Playboy Club filled our week. This last place, the Playboy Club, took only a short flight up to Lake Geneva. The neighbor of Steve's parents owned two planes including his own private airstrip on his back lawn of about five acres. I was in Big Money Ville.

The date was 1970. The thought of two young men, in their early 20's, entering those sacred doors of the Playboy Club, where beautiful scantly dressed women ran around serving food and drinks, definitely would be a highlight of our trip to Chicago.

Steve's mother set up the trip. The neighbor was generous in his offering to take us. Right before we left I ate a tuna fish sandwich and drank a glass of milk. Moms always want their young sons to have plenty of energy before visiting Playboy Clubs across the country.

We took the short walk across the grassy fields and met the neighbor. He took us to his plane and we entered. The small Cessna had been sitting in the warm sun all morning. As we entered I guessed the cockpit temperature to be around 105 degrees. The interior was covered with a fluffy white substance. The material looked like the fur of an albino Alaskan husky. It fit the lifestyle of those who lived in this neighborhood.

We took off with Steve in the front seat with the pilot while I remained in the back surrounded by albino husky. Before we set our course to the land of fantasy the pilot asked Steve,

"Do you want to view your house from a different angle?"

I am sure Steve did not know what he meant, and neither did I.

"Sure", he answered.

No sooner did he get the words out of his mouth, the neighbor dipped the left wing straight down and we were looking at Steve's mother at a 90-degree angle from the side window. She waved at us from the yard.

The thing about doing such maneuvers in a plane concerns the stomach. It also does the same maneuver. My stomach, just recently filled with a tuna fish sandwich and a glass of milk, had just been turned upside down in a 105-degree cockpit.

As the plane straightened out and flew north, I glanced around at this plane's beautiful interior and wondered how it would look with a lunch deposit. I also started searching for something to make the deposit into just in case the situation arose. I eventually found a large manila envelope containing maps. I emptied the maps and set the envelope to the side for safety.

The flight to the Playboy Club remained uneventfully for the most part with a few bumpy air pockets. I settled down in my stomach by the time we approached the landing strip at Lake Geneva. I think the pilot had a thing about showing off his skills to anyone who could see him. Before we landed he once again dropped the left wing 90 degrees towards the ground and again my lunch did the same.

This time, when he pulled out of the turn and started to land, the outcome went through a change. I am thankful I searched the cabin after takeoff because I now could contain the tuna fish sandwich and milk into the envelope and not onto the albino husky fur interior.

We exited the plane. No one knew what happened to me.

Steve asked, "What's in the envelope?"

I gave him my best answer. "Lunch."

I headed toward the closest trash container to complete my task. I felt fairly good about the fact no damage to the interior of the plane took place. As I reached the bin, the envelope, which by now was soaked through, gave way and the secret was out. The nearby attendants said not to worry. They would clean up the mess. We headed off to the club. I still felt dizzy and not completely recovered from the ordeal.

Here I was, in the prime of my youth, entering the House of Fantasy that Hugh Heffner built. The restaurant presented just as it appeared in all the Playboy magazines college men buy to keep them focused on the end goal. Get a good job, making a lot of money and all this can by yours. You too can be a key holder and live the dream. Hugh was really onto something. He built an empire around men buying into this idea of success.

I remained too sick to enjoy the hour we spent having a drink. All I could do was drink a coke to help settle my stomach. I barely noticed the long legs and full busts, bunny tails included. I guess this idea of success held little value for me because the visit became my first and last to Heff's dream palace.

Chapter 10
Europe

Steve and I booked a flight from Chicago to New York. We tried to find a car rental dealer who needed two wild and crazy post-college men to drive a car to NY for them. We struck out.

Because we happened to be typical UCSB graduates in the late 60s and early 70s, we each carried small amounts of marijuana in bags left over from our recreational habits. We felt a little uncomfortable traveling with the weed in its' leaf form. What does any typical young adult from the 60s do in this situation? Make brownies of course.

Airplane travel in the 70s is now remembered as a totally different experience from today. No baggage checks with x-ray machines on domestic flights and carry-on bags remained with the passenger untouched. Shoes stayed on our feet and we brought as many liquids and other forms of pastes and gels we wanted. Even the flight on Icelandic Airlines to the capital of Reykjavik produced no security checks.

This is a brave new world today and travel has become much more challenging. Most of the demands are just to get on the plane. Travel restrictions remain the one freedom I am sorry we lost due to world conflicts and the inability for countries to coexist in the world.

We landed in Iceland after a flight throughout the night. We booked a hotel to stay for a day and explore this island of beautiful blond Vikings. Norsemen populated and colonized this country in the middle of the Atlantic, centuries ago and it appeared they did a good job. We checked into our hotel and found a tour bus leaving in an hour to take people to one of the last land based whaling stations in the world. We loaded onto the bus with other tourists. We had started our world travel adventure on an island in the middle of nowhere.

Iceland is a fishing and tourism country. Today they are energy independent due to the many geothermal plants throughout the island. In 1970 one saw the hot water pipes coming into town providing the population with hot water and heating. There are many other geothermal locations in the world along the "Ring of Fire" able to produce the same result. In the field of using natural heat energy, Iceland leads the way.

The drive to the whaling station took us through a tundra-like landscape, past herds of Icelandic horses and steam smoke, rising from fissures surrounding the countryside. As we pulled into the station I noticed a whaling ship arriving at the docks towing three whales of different sizes. Within minutes the bodies of these magnificent mammals were lifted onto the cutting slab. The slicing and dicing began soon after our arrival. Within an hour only the bones remained. The blubber and other usable parts soon disappeared and were sent to the industries using whale meat.

I had no idea whale meat was found in things like dog food and other products probably synthetically made today. I took no political stance regarding whaling in 1970. Icelanders, living on this island, were fishermen. What I observed supported how they lived. Whaling is a hot topic today and the demand for whale products has lessened. If the whale population ever returns to the non-endangered list, the whales, including myself will be happy.

The next day our flight to Luxembourg from Reykjavik left early in the morning and soon we looked down from the plane onto the continent of Europe. We landed and were directed towards customs. Steve and I noticed something we did not see in Iceland. Uniformed officers seemed to be going through the baggage of certain passengers. They chose the ones who appeared suspicious in some way. Most of those pulled aside wore their hair long. All of them appeared young. We wore our hair long. We were young. We carried brownies. We could be in deep shit.

I said to Steve, "Quick, let's get into this bathroom and get rid of the brownies."

Both of us ducked into the WC and discussed our situation. We chose from two options, flush our treats or eat them. The decision became one of doing both. Not knowing how many brownies we could eat and concerned about throwing away our special snack, we ate three-quarters of them. Reluctantly we flushed the rest. As we departed the bathroom with our luggage, another surprise awaited us. We went through customs and they didn't stop us.

"Can you believe this?" I asked Steve. "They never checked our bags."

I was glad we played it safe. I held no thoughts that our first night in Europe, beginning soon would never be forgotten.

We quickly found a hotel for the night and checked in. Within 20 minutes after unpacking, we realized too many brownies were consumed. We needed to get out of the hotel and walk off the effects of this baked Mexican weed. Somehow we stumbled across a nightclub act featuring girls doing nude and provocative acts. I missed out at the Playboy Club in Lake Geneva but at age twenty-five, I chose not to pass on this show.

We exchanged money at the airport so both of us held the right currency to get in. The problem confronting us stemmed from our inability to communicate. Asking the entrance price remained beyond our ability. The only act possible was to hold out a pile of bills and hope the ticket person took the correct amount. We entered the nightclub. I quickly realized something. Europe and where I sat at the moment contained little resemblance to Kansas. Here we were in a foreign land and Dorothy was nowhere to be found.

The club contained individual tables seating two to four people. Customers ordered food and drinks while different acts performed on stage. The waitresses also played a part in the show. They waited on tables but also went off into the back rooms with different clients. Most of the audience appeared to be wealthy businessmen. Each one wore a coat and tie. Twenty minutes later the gentlemen, who visited the backrooms, would emerge and leave the nightclub. The waitress would come out later and continue serving drinks and food or whatever else she recommended on the side.

This introduction to the nightlife became my first exposure to the sexual openness existing in Europe. Steve and I sat at our table and sipped beers all night. The girls, serving food and drinks, never approached us. They realized we were beyond any communication. Our only action possible, watch the show, sip beer and let time pass until the effects of the brownies wore off. Around two a.m. we walked back to our hotel, flopped on our beds and fell asleep. Our first night in Europe remained under our belt.

Chapter 11
When in Europe

Steve, never having been to Europe before, seemed to accept the differences between the two worlds. We both enjoyed eating the cuisine in France and Germany. Embracing a certain truth in travel helped us both to enjoy the experience.

'When in Europe do as the Europeans do.'

This statement is one of necessity. It can make or break a travel journey, no matter where you go.

The above statement became evident when we visited two college friends, both stationed in Europe serving in the U.S. army. We first visited Jack and his wife on an army base near Karlsruhe, Germany. Army bases in Europe are like small towns. Movie theaters, restaurants, bowling alleys and PX shopping provided the military families with everything they need. They never have to leave the base.

Jack and his wife lived the above choice. They never traveled around Germany on days off, always eating at home or at a restaurant on base. Jack's wife became an avid member of the bridge club playing most afternoons. She hated her life in Europe and shared nothing positive regarding the German people. She did not want to learn the language or anything about the culture. Her intent focused on their return to the states as soon as the tour ended.

Our other friend, Richard, stationed in West Berlin, lived a different lifestyle. In order to visit him, Steve and I needed to drive across the border into East Germany and enter West Berlin at one of the checkpoints. While driving through East Germany, our car could not pull over and stop along the guarded road. At the border into West Berlin, the East German guards did not make the crossing an experience worth repeating. Military men and women grabbed passports out of our hands, yelled at us in German and attempted to make entering West Berlin as uncomfortable as possible.

Rich and his wife lived on an army base with easy access to West Berlin and the German culture. As soon as Rich finished work he returned home, removed his uniform and changed into civilian clothing. He and his wife went out to dinner, ate the German food and learned to speak a little of the language.

They did not participate in bridge clubs or any of the programs set up for those families choosing to remain on base during their tour. Rich and his wife loved their stay in Berlin, which happened to be in one of most controversial places in post-WWII Europe. Becoming a part of their surrounding environment and taking full advantage of the opportunity the army tour provided, gave both Rich and his wife a gift each would be able to cherish forever.

During our visit with Rich, Steve and I went over to Eastern Berlin several times, crossing at a famous border called Check Point Charlie. The transition from the western part of the city into the eastern sector became an eye opener. Berlin was heavily bombed during the war. The western region of Berlin, after the war, held an occupation force of England, the U.S. and France. The city went through a complete facelift including new buildings and thriving businesses. Employment was high and the atmosphere electric with a nightlife scene and full entertainment.

The eastern sector presented a culture of devastation and gloom. Many of the buildings looked exactly like they did following WWII. The people walked around in drab clothing and showed no sign of life in their step. They looked like an oppressed people under the Soviet domination.

The Berlin Wall built nine years before 1970, still remained in place. This monumental eyesore separated the differences between the Berlin of the west and the Berlin of the east. One culture ruled by two separate governments. The diversities were enormous. The Eastern powers ruling East Berlin did not want their citizens exposed to the capitalist lifestyle of the west.

When the wall finally came down in 1990, experiencing the moment was one of great celebration for those living there. Had I been in Berlin at the time, I would have obtained a souvenir of the famous barrier. There must be pieces of the concrete divider, covered in graffiti, on fireplace mantles throughout Germany and Europe. The cement chunks serve to remind Europeans of the terrible time when Berlin and Germany remained divided.

Chapter 12
Education in Europe

Our main focus for going to Europe was to get jobs in a skiing area, work, ski for the winter and continue to travel in the spring. My intent was to stay abroad longer than Steve and remain in Europe. I lived in Salzburg before and I fell in love with the diversity of the continent.

Before winter set in we both visited Austria and the family with whom I lived with for almost a year. Six years passed since my stay with the Mastnak family. Both of the young daughters were grown up. Monica became a hairdresser and Sonja continued school to complete her education.

During my stay with the family and my year as a student in Bundesrealgymnasium (all one word), I came home with a positive attitude towards the European system of education. I did not know at the time, but I would later spend 22 years working for the American education system in California and Arizona.

Bundesrealgymnasium is the name of the school I attended. It took me several weeks before I could pronounce it correctly.

In 1963 most of the high schools in Austria were not co-educational. This meant fewer distractions for the young men in the gymnasium and any competition for the attention of the young female students, living in Salzburg, took place at the many social events scheduled on the weekends. Yes, just like La Jolla, Salzburg taught ballroom dancing and held dinner parties to prepare their youth for society.

When students in Europe reach the age of twelve, they take a screening test in school. The test determines if they are able to continue in the field of higher learning. If a student does not qualify to continue, he or she must choose a profession in which they choose to be trained. Examples of such occupations include hairdressing, electrician, auto mechanic, and hotel management.

Students in these work fields can spend up to four years studying as an apprentice and taking classes. Subjects are used to teach them what they will need to perform the job. If a student is training to be an electrician, math and the use of tools is taught. If a hairdresser is the desired work, I am sure the same material is covered much like a Beauty College in the U.S.

The students work at job locations for their training. Hotel management would find the young apprentice learning all there is to know about running such an establishment while actually working at an Inn. He could train in the kitchen or learn the business side of hotel work. It took three or four years to complete the course and when the student graduated he or she already had years of training under their belt.

There seemed to be a level of management among the young workers. Those apprentices, in their last year of training, managed the beginning workers. This system allowed the owners more time to run the business and not have to keep an eye on the beginners.

Salaries were paid according to the year each student reached in their training. With each additional year, the student's wages increased. After the apprentices completed their education and skill tests, they are given a certificate qualifying them to work anywhere in Europe in their field. They now possessed a skill and they are only seventeen years old. How about that America?

In the U.S. many students would rather learn a trade and earn money while getting their training. Instead, they continually fall through the cracks of our education system. They are forced to attend a school they have little interest in and are exposed to subjects holding little value in their life. I used the word exposed because those who care little about school do not learn these subjects.

I went to school, in La Jolla, with young men who were lobster fishers. They would get up in the early hours, set their traps or check them before coming to school. Others worked in the construction industry on weekends and did jobs in which they could earn an income while in school. These students cared little about World History, Geometry and all those other classes they would never use in their careers.

Today I see the same type of students in high schools throughout California and Arizona. They are usually the ones in detention, acting out in class and selling dope in the school parking lots in order to make money. They receive diminutive guidance as to what they can do in life. Many come from families barely making it financially. Employment is what they seek and experience to go with a job.

Many of these students drop out before finishing high school, possessing few skills as they enter the workforce. Some end up flipping burgers at fast food restaurants. Those who do graduate, but have no interest in college, are also in this situation. They are not trained in any field. Many go to tech schools or community colleges and learn a trade. Teachers and principals spend large amounts of time dealing with the acting out behaviors of these young people who do not want to be at school.

There is a choice we must make in this country. We can continue forcing a high school education on every child, even though some are not able to do the work or want to do the work. At age eighteen these young adults continue to enter into the work force with limited skills. The alternative is a new system directing those who are slipping through the cracks into an apprentice program at age twelve or thirteen. They would learn a skill preparing them for the workforce at age eighteen.

Education in America is the elephant in the room no one is talking about. The elephant is getting bigger every year. The above plan works. We can have a nation with a workforce trained in a skilled profession or burger flippers surviving on minimal salaries. The clock is ticking. Tick, tick, tick.

Chapter 13
Third World Countries

After visiting our two friends in the military, Steve and I headed to a part of Austria containing a ski resort catering to English tourists. My ability to speak German and wait tables provided me with a job in a hotel called the Drei Morran in the Austrian town of Lermoos. The name of the Inn translates to "The Three Wise Men". When I tried to find the hotel with Google, it did not appear. New owners may have changed the name or someone with a lot of money purchased it for their own residence.

Steve was hired to work with the maintenance department. We didn't start work until December so we headed off to Spain and Morocco to catch the last sunshine of fall and observe how Franco treated the Spanish.

Spain became a blur of museums and bullfights. We met up with two young ladies Steve knew from San Jose State. They were touring Europe as well and we decided to travel through Spain and Morocco with them. One was an art major so the trips to the many museums became an educational experience for all of us. The bullfights, however, convinced me this part of the Spanish culture I'd rather not participate in. I am not Ernest Hemingway and the slaughter was beyond my comfort zone.

After a short tour in Spain, we headed across the Straits of Gibraltar and entered the continent of Africa. Morocco is a third world country. It also has a modern city Humphrey Bogart made famous. "Here's looking at you' kid" and "Play it again Sam" put Casablanca on the

Hollywood map. Movie watchers probably visit the city every year and try to relive the magic of the film. Piano bars in the city must get call outs from the audience requesting a replay of the last song even though the man on the keys is not really Sam. Do they still make white tuxedos?

The first city we landed in was Tangiers. This is one of the two border towns where one can enter when coming across from Spain. The main part of this North African metropolis felt like a city trying to enter the twentieth century. Cars and shops lined the streets and tourism appeared to be the main focus. Most shops sold all those things one would expect to find in Morocco. Clothing, brass knives, and lamps, like the one in the Aladdin movie, could be found in the merchant's stalls.

As we walked around the main shopping section of Tangiers, hustlers, or tour guides, as they preferred to be called, approached us offering the best price for anything we wanted. Several of them kept asking us,

"Have you been to the Medina yet?"

Steve and I had no idea what they were talking about because the word Medina meant nothing to us. Finally, we conceded and asked one of the 'tour guides' to take us to the Medina.

Moroccan towns seem to be separated by two time periods. The main sector is trying to become modern like their European neighbors to the North. It is filled with the items made in Europe as well as clothing a shopper may find in stores throughout the African continent.

The other section of town wants to hold onto the old world and its' roots. This is the Medina. Its' location is almost a secret and we needed a guide to take us there. We were led to a gateway, through a wall, which seemed to penetrate the two different worlds. What existed on the other side would participate in my decision to travel and see the world.

As we entered the realm of the Medina we entered a world unchanged in 2000 years. The rutted out dirt streets were overrun with donkeys carrying goods to the storeowners. The roads remained too narrow for trucks and any modern transport vehicles. People dressed in the robes and clothing which appeared much the same as the attire worn in movies portraying the life of Christ. We had traveled back in time and all of us loved it.

I almost expected to see Ali Baba walking down the street holding a lamp and offering to sell it to us. Old men with beards sat in front of their shops, sipping mint tea, selling cloth, and brass items engraved with different designs found throughout North Africa.

Butcher shops contained mostly goat carcasses. Goat meat made up the main protein section of the Moroccan diet. This relative to sheep seemed to be the national animal of Morocco. They were everywhere. Herds of them came down the street and buyers would shout out a price for one of them, thus buying the evening meal for the family. The Medina pulsated life and walking through it the traveler could experience the heartbeat of the North African world.

We shopped in this ancient world for a few hours and finally decided to return to our hotel. The modern world awaiting us on the other side of the wall but I could have easily stayed longer in the ancient Medina.

The more I traveled throughout Morocco my desire to visit other countries just as old increased. I hope the Medina's' in all the towns of the Arab world continue for tourists, like myself, to walk through. It was another world.

Having a car and the freedom to drive where we wanted, took us to many of the Moroccan towns and cities I read about in my World Geography studies. Fez, the city from which some people believe the three wise men traveled, appeared on our travel route. It had been a city, years before, where science and astrology were taught and practiced. Fez was the leader in stargazing and planet alignment studies in the ancient world.

In 1970 Fez held little from its' days of science and glory. Hustlers met tourists as they departed from their car or bus and many of the buildings were in need of repair. It was no longer on a major trade route and the city seemed to be slowly disappearing beneath the desert sands.

Casablanca, a modern Moroccan city, still held a touch of the French colonial imprint. We stayed one night. We looked forward to visiting other towns containing the ancient flavor of North Africa and the Arab world.

Marrakech, made famous in song by Crosby, Stills, Nash and Young, became our next destination. We arrived at the walled city in our own Marrakech Express. The Opal station wagon, purchased in Germany when Steve and I first arrived in Europe, showed signs of rust throughout the floor and side panels. It remained our steed throughout this desert country.

Marrakech at once became my favorite city in Morocco. The outside walls still stood intact and sturdy as though they could withstand any raid from the camel armies of centuries past. It was in this city I found the one item I desired in Morocco more than anything else. Gulamean beads. I do not know where the name came from but when I researched the beads, Google called them Venetian North Africa trade beads.

A side note is appropriate at this moment. I referred to Google a second time in my quest to find where the word Gulamean came from. This is the edit for the second edition of Living Beneath the Radar. Google refers anyone who looks up the word Gulamean to Living Beneath the Radar by Jeffrey R Crimmel. It seems I have created a word and have given it meaning.

In history, before any currency was created, trade beads from many different countries were used as currency. Beads, worn by the women of the family, showed off their wealth. The females were the walking Banks of the ancient world.

These beads, made by glass blowers in Venice, Italy, were much desired by collectors, like myself, who first saw them in California boutiques and head shops. I did not want to buy beads in a store in Berkley or Santa Barbara. I wanted to buy the beads in North Africa. They could be found in the markets as a tourist item.

I eventually found someone who owned a strand and wanted to sell it. I was obliged to drink a glass of tea and go through the process required for any transaction made in this part of the world. Not to bargain for any item purchased would be an insult to the merchant. In the movie 'The Life of Brian', the word haggle is used to mean bargain.

I loved shopping this way. Can you imagine business conducted in this manner in a department store like Macys? Haggling over the price of a pair of designer shoes, while drinking tea, would bring the retail world of America to a halt. Tea consumption would double or triple and the need for more bathrooms in department stores would increase.

The strand of beads was finally paid for. I returned to where my travel partners waited and I divided the beads between all four of us. They rejoiced with my discovery. I wore my beads around my neck until the leather cord finally broke while body surfing in Goa, India, several years later. If the strand ever washes up on the beach in Goa, some anthropologist may wonder how Venetian North African trade beads made their way to India.

By this time, in our African travels, the two young ladies from California experienced enough of this male-dominated culture. They lost interest in traveling further into the African continent. Going to the camel market in Mauritania, remained out of their comfort zone.

Steve felt our travel adventure got side tracked by women with little desire for the unknown. We headed north to Spain to return the ladies to their car. They wanted to travel to Scandinavia and visit a civilization they could relate to.

One last adventure unfolded on our return to the European continent. We kept getting flat tires in Morocco and we could not understand why. We would purchase a tire appearing to have good tread and drive for several hundred miles before it gave out. Our last visit to a tire store, before taking the ferry to Spain, gave us the answer.

A tire, needing replacement, was removed from the rim and stacked with mountains of other tires filling the shop. The flat tire still had good tread but it seemed a little thin. I could push my finger into the tire with ease.

You cannot do that with a tire made in Europe. We were told it would take 20 minutes to change the tire so Steve and I decided to walk around the shop.

As we came around a pile of rubber wheels, we found out how the Moroccans get good mileage out of their Firestones. An old man and a boy sat on the ground each holding a special knife. They were taking tires, whose tread seemed rather flat, and carving new tread into the tires. Each carver followed the old patterns on the tire using particular care. When they finished the tire looked almost brand new with deep new grooves for the road. The finished product would make even the Michelin Man envious.

We knew then, upon our return to Europe, new used tires needed to be purchased. We still faced many miles of driving and a tire, re-grooved in Morocco, would not fit our safety standards.

Chapter 14
Working in Europe

Winter approached and our jobs in Austria would soon begin. We said our goodbyes to our female companions in France and headed towards Austria. We drove through Europe picking up hitchhikers at the different Youth Hostels where we stayed. Most were willing to help with the high fuel expenses thus making the trip less of a financial burden.

We arrived at the Drei Morran Hotel before the first snow. Lermoos is a small village near the border of Germany and in the winter the population caters to skiing tourists from all over the world. The kitchen staff at the hotel trained young apprentices ranging from entry level to master cooks. The owner of the hotel ran the kitchen and his ex-wife managed the hotel. Most of the workers came from different parts of Austria and lived in the dorm rooms provided for them during the winter season.

I did not receive training in Europe to be a waiter, even though I worked in the field for several years in Santa Barbara and Lake Tahoe. I had to work under a master waiter as his bus boy. He presented as a friendly young man, around nineteen years old and interested in America and the Wild West. As the winter progressed he asked me everything I knew about cowboys and where the buffalo roam. He even purchased my cowboy boots I brought to Europe, as well as a few other clothing items similar to something a cowboy might wear.

We both worked long hours, usually during breakfast and dinner. At lunchtime Steve and I were off. We would have skied but the snows did not fall that year. The winter passed Austria in 1970-1971 with terrible snow conditions. Afternoons were spent exploring the town and visiting nearby Garmisch-Partenkirchen in Germany. The U.S. army maintained a small military base there. Being American citizens gave us access to the PX.

In January winter set in and some snow began to fall. English tours arrived and filling the local hotels. Skiing remained at a low due to lack of snow but the English knew how to accommodate. They stayed up all night drinking and cutting loose. They were away from England and when the English party they seem to do so like there is no tomorrow.

For many of the English tourists, tomorrow did not begin until 2 or 3 in the afternoon due to the large amounts of alcohol consumed the night before. The English proved to be quite fun. They found my American accent interesting and my story as to how I arrived in Europe fascinating. This became a real ego booster.

Working the late shift kept me up until 3:00 in the morning serving drinks. I still needed to set up for breakfast at 7 am and help serve the early birds. Jobs in Europe do not restrict those filling them with 8-hour shifts. A person labored in the area he or she trained for as long as needed. These were the hours I observed at the Drei Morran. I assume there are periods of time, after the season is finished when the workers are without a salary. Hopefully, they have put money away for these non-income periods.

Chapter 15
Spring 1971

Towards the end of the ski season, Steve and I started to get itchy feet. We left the hotel in April and headed to the areas of Europe reported having received snow. Switzerland is the snow capital of Europe. A few places in France also reported a good snowfall.

In St. Moritz, Switzerland in the 70s, fur coats seemed to be the rage among the rich. While walking around town I recognized the whole cat family represented on the backs of wealthy long-legged women. Leopard, tiger, and lynx were just a few of the felines on display. The ladies, strutting around town, showed these animals in a whole different manner. Today I hope the consciousness of Europe has been elevated to the level where this practice is no longer tolerated.

In France one of the Youth Hostels where we stayed served a meal I have never seen before. The dish turned out to be rabbit brain. It must have been a delicacy. The brain was served alone with vegetables on the side and left nothing to the imagination. It was gray and possessed all the patterns and designs of a brain, distinguishing it from other meat dishes. We must have eaten it because both Steve and I sampled all the cuisine in the countries we visited.

The Matterhorn and Mt. Blanc remain as must- see wonders of France and Switzerland. Tourists flock to them in the thousands. The most beautiful place we stayed in all of Europe happened to be the Youth Hostel in Grindelwald, Switzerland. This place became so sought after one could only stay for two nights to make room for all the other travelers who wanted to also experience this high altitude village.

Grindelwald is located across the valley from Mt. Eiger, famous for its' sheer rock face attracting climbers and other crazy thrill-seekers each year. The sloping pristine meadows on the hills surrounding the village are filled with quaint Swiss Chalets. These were once the hospitals and recovery lodgings for victims of different breathing disorders in the 1800s and early 1900s. Now they are the homes of the wealthy making the journey to this high altitude locale every summer.

Climbing the face of the Eiger is a feat which needs two or three days. Nights found climbers in suspended beds dangling above the valley floor thousands of feet below. A climber needed to be sure the spike he pounded into the rock held him and his bed safely for the night. Accidents happen in mountain climbing and those on the Eiger were usually fatal. The expression, 'different strokes for different folks', would apply here. Climbing the Eiger remains, to this day, not a stroke for this folk.

*****

We finished our ski season in the country of Andorra, located in the Pyrenees Mountains between Spain and France. Because Andorra is a tax-free nation, shoppers from both neighboring borders made the capital a place of destination. Shoppers came to buy those high priced items saving hundreds of extra dollars or Francs in tax charged in their own countries. Spanish and French are spoken throughout Andorra as well as Basque, the language of the people living in the region.

The Basque people desire to be independent of Spain. They continue their fight to keep their language and customs intact. They do not want to be assimilated into the surrounding cultures and countries dominating the area. Basques are famous for their ability to raise sheep. Shepherds from this region can be found in California and Arizona.

I lived in Flagstaff, AZ for ten years. The Basque lived there since the 1800s. A Basque shepherd took a large flock of sheep across the deserts of California and Arizona finding the cool, higher elevations of Flagstaff perfect for grazing. The impact on the local wildlife competing for the same grasses is a topic of discussion played out in the history of this area.

A large flock of sheep still makes the trip up to the national forests of Flagstaff from the lower elevations of the Verde Valley in the summer and back down to lower elevations in winter. I have seen the flock once while driving down to the valley on highway 17 back in 2002. I am sure it is a Basque shepherd herding the flock.

If you come to Flagstaff and take one of the many tours describing the history of the area, one quickly finds out about the legacy left by the shepherds. Aspen trees, throughout the countryside, are engraved with the letters the lonely shepherds wrote to each other, along with the dates of the messages. The trees are considered historical landmarks and I believe protected from being cut down.

Chapter 16
Summer 1971

Summer approached and both Steve and I prepared to find some sun. Before leaving Spain a side trip to the island of Ibiza, off the coast of the Balearic Islands, seemed in order. The island in 1971 was just starting to realize the tourist potential. Hippies inhabited the capital, also called Ibiza. They lived in small hotels in the old town while constructions of high-rise luxury towers took place near the city. Many, in this generation of the 70s, purchased shops and restaurants in order to accommodate the needs and desires of the European flower community.

We both toured the old fort on the island and stayed for a few nights enjoying the music and food prepared in organic restaurants. Pot seemed available which surprised both of us due to the tight government of Franco and his security police force.

On a photo side trip around the island, Steve and I came across a walled in container holding dirt and other items deposited from a nearby church. I climbed onto the mound of trash in order to gain some height for a picture of the old fort across the way. As I walked around on the pile of dirt, objects, white in color, could be seen protruding out of the earth mounds. With a little digging, both Steve and I discovered what we were standing on. Bones. Not only limbs and feet but also skulls were found in the heap. Not wanting to miss a photo opportunity and not holding much more respect for the remains than the church who put them in the trash, we started to do a photo shoot holding a few of the skulls next to our own heads and moving the jaws up and down as a ventriloquist would do when operating their dummy.

After a few pictures, we climbed out of the recycle container and started to piece together the mystery of the bones in relationship to the church. A graveyard lay on the other side of a wall and being a small island, the land available for the burial site remained small. We reasoned the bones were dug up and deposited in the trash after being buried for a number of years. More room was needed for the newly departed whose family had the money for burial needs. These were old body remains removed and placed in a trash bin so the church could resell the burial sites to the next generation. This explanation is the only conclusion we could come up with. I will now leave the mystery of the bones to rest. Get it? Bones to rest.

We heard from the local youth of Ibiza the islands of Greece sported some of the best beaches and inexpensive lifestyles in Europe. Cheap living would keep us from having to find work anytime soon. I did not know at the time but Greece held the key, giving me incentive to head east and beyond.

Traveling along the coast of France, we encountered much of the wealth of Europe. Plush estates dotted the coastline with the inhabitants keeping their Francs and Marks in the banks of Monaco. The money institutions probably gave them high-interest rates to hold their currency. The banks could then lend out the money to the gamblers and high rollers participating in the casino's activities.

Italy, the next country we passed through, held treasures of the past. We stopped at Florence to see how David was doing. We visited Rome, walking through the stadium built by the Romans. Pompeii demonstrated the problems of living too close to a volcano. The city of Bari is the port where we caught the ferry that took us to Greece.

Before leaving Italy I must revisit our trip to Florence. A special insight into my life occurred there and even to this day I am not been able to make complete sense of what happened.

*****

About a year before I started out on this journey, I dreamt repeatedly about my life as a boy, living in a farmhouse. I did not know where the dream took place and I did not give the vision much thought.

A college friend of ours had a brother living outside of Florence. He studied classical guitar at a school in the city. Jim, our college friend, told us his brother would be happy to put us up for a few days. We were given directions where he lived outside of Florence and we drove there and found the place easily.

As we arrived at the house and got out of the car, I froze. I knew the house well. I lived here as a young boy in my repeating dream. We found out later the home used to be a farmhouse and was over 400 years old. The building, now converted into several apartments, remained on the exterior as it did 400 years before. I believe Italy passed laws protecting old structures from any changes to the outside. This reason allowed me to recognize the farmhouse as we drove up to it.

I discovered, after repeating the dream story to Steve, when one shares an experience with others, you might not get the response expected. Steve told me,

"I think you had a synapse leap."

I tried to understand what he meant but the description of synapse leap made little sense. I dreamt about living in this house repeatedly for over a year and even remembered feeding the chickens. The house contained the same stairway leading up to the living quarters. The only thing missing seemed to be my ability to speak Italian.

I did not research 'synapse leap' for two reasons. First, Steve graduated in economics and not as a psychologist. Second, I determined my experience would remain mine. Letting someone dismiss the dream with a term like 'synapse leap' in order to feel comfortable because western thinking could not explain the vision, was not going to happen. After we stayed at the farmhouse, the dream never reoccurred.

Shirley Maclean, where were you in 1971?

A few years later, when I lived in India and started to read different books about the religions of the East, I finally received an explanation for the dreams. Hinduism, Buddhism and other offshoots of these ancient religious practices believe in reincarnation. When people have an experience like mine, including revisiting a place lived in a previous life, Eastern thought does not negate the vision or dream with psycho-babble. They respect the experience and honor it as well.

The western religions are new compared to the religions of the East. The West holds onto some rigid thought processes excluding the supernatural or people remembering past lives. Such experiences are written about and accepted in the East. Many books are full of stories telling of people remembering past lives.

This was my experience. I do not plan to return to the farmhouse even if I could find it. I am now able to lay the dreams to rest. My only regret is I cannot speak Italian in this life. It is such a beautiful language.

The trip through Italy took us to Rome, the town of many ruins. The Coliseum and the workings of the animal cages beneath the arena floor became most fascinating to me. I sometimes wonder about the games played in the States and the names given to the teams competing for the honor of defeating each other. Bears, Lions, Bengal Tigers, and Panthers seem to serve notice of a team's strength. These same animals were probably used in the battles with Gladiators and later on to provide entertainment for Roman citizens as followers of the upstart religion called Christianity were put to death.

Pompeii is also a city worth seeing and it also held the secrets of how the early Roman citizens lived. Water canals to supply plumbing for homes and even hot water for bathhouses were found among the preserved ruins. Because the city lay beneath the layers of volcanic ash for centuries, it has become one of the most visited sites for tourists to see what a Roman town looked like years before.

Steve and I wanted to get to the white sands of Greece as the weather started to warm so we headed towards the east coast of Italy and the port city of Bari. From there we could catch a ferry to our next destination along with our trusty Opal, still in one piece, rust and all.

The ferryboat from Bari dropped us off at Corfu, an island off the Greek mainland. The weather, finally warming up, felt good. We started to dig out our lighter clothing from our suitcases to wear as we traveled through this hospitable country. We looked at the map of

Europe and saw the islands of Greece extending even further south into the Mediterranean Sea.

The Greeks are a great seafaring nation and from the main port of Piraeus, which is near Athens, ships left daily connecting to all those islands. Boats brought supplies and tourists to the white washed towns lining the coastlines.

Many islands exist in Greece. Choosing only one to visit can be difficult. Even though 38 years has passed since I traveled in Greece, life probably remains unchanged in the small villages. Fishing and farming is the main source of income. Tourism is the industry for most Greeks in the summer. This is especially true if the village is located on one of the many islands visited each summer by the European countries to the north.

Greek traffic jam seen from our car

When summer arrives in Greece the fishermen take on the job of transporting the tourists from the towns to the many beaches surrounding the different islands. They still fish in the evenings or early mornings after all the tourists are taken to the beaches or returned to their hotels. They sleep on their boats for a few hours and continue the routine the next day.

Greeks work especially hard to please Americans and Europeans coming to experience the most beautiful island nation in the Mediterranean. When the summer season is over, cool winds blow down from Europe as winter approaches. Many of the shops, open in the summer, close down and the communities return to their pace of life. Winters may find the residents sitting by the warm fires, playing with their Worry Beads and recalling the many stories acted out during the summer. These stories may include tales of the American youth, trying to demonstrate how much Ouzo or Retzina they can drink. The summers in Greece give the local residents much-needed income and plenty to laugh about during the winter.

The first islands Steve and I went to were Mykonos and Ios. Both of these places had beautiful beaches and white-washed buildings with blue trim. Most of the structures appeared as though they were painted yesterday. There is a law in Greece stating the homes and work residents need to be white- washed every year and kept in perfect photo card condition. Tourism is a serious business in Greece and unkempt walls and residential homes are not permitted.

The famous windmills on Mykonos are included in the strict maintenance laws. When the afternoon breezes blew, the sails of the windmills unfurled and spun in motion for the tourists to photograph and video for their relatives back home. These windmills are beautiful to watch. I even understand wind power is making a comeback.

Mykonos is also the island one mostly sees when opening a brochure of Greece. It is the playland of the European rich communities. Almost all the beaches allow nudity. There is even a beach containing mostly Gay men and women. The tourists population would meet on the beach, chat and have fun rubbing sun tan lotion on each other. If a connection or interest developed, the couple would head off towards one of the many boulders filling the surrounding hillsides. A more physical connection could be made, away from the eyes of other sunbathers or the Greek families who owned and ran the restaurants at the beaches.

Most Greeks are devout Orthodox Christians. They only put up with nudity on the hot sands. Clothing is required when lunchtime arrived.

Steve and I left Mykonos after a week and traveled to the island of Ios. We heard this was an island catering especially to young backpack travelers. Visitors could pitch their tents on the beach, play on the hot sands, swim in the crystal clear water and spend their money in the nearby town. Ios was exactly how I described it. Restaurants, one on each end of the beach, served a breakfast of bread, yogurt, and eggs to the tent population. Afternoons usually included swimming in the ocean or learning to play the guitar in order to impress the next group of young women arriving from the boats daily.

Nights found the tent population doing exactly what they did the night before. Many said they would not repeat the previous night but they had short memories. The beer, Ouzo and other Greek alcohol mixtures flowed until the early morning. I am still amazed how the beach people, under the influence of a night of drinking, walked down the dirt road from town each night, safely returning to their tents a quarter mile away.

After a week of this lifestyle the pull of travel and seeing the world directed me to move on. Steve seemed to be in his element. He did not want to expand his world experiences. Wine, women, and song satisfied how he wanted to spend the summer and so we parted ways. I headed back to the car in Athens and drove off towards Turkey. The excitement of visiting the country and people who separated Europe from Asia held more interest than the constant party on Ios. I loved traveling to the unknown.

Chapter 17
Turkey

During my first trip to Turkey, I picked up several Americans in Athens. Their travel time in Europe stretched six months longer than my time away from the States. It seemed travelers who have been away from America the longest possess the most clout. They seemed to know more about ways to get around Europe than those who just arrived. The first thing they showed me was how to raise money. They took me to the local hospital to sell blood, something in great demand in Greece.

Giving blood is against church laws for Greeks. Because Greeks did not give blood the demand put the price at around $20. This amount was good money for travelers in 1971. I am not sure how the Greeks, who received blood from alcohol mixed donations, felt after they were given the blood. I would not be surprised if some blood recipients suffered a hangover the next day and wondered how that happened.

One of the American travelers with me carried a lot of weight on his football player sized frame. He wanted to make a little extra money before going to Turkey. He thought, because of his body weight, he could sell another pint of blood the next day in Thessaloniki, on the way to Turkey. We accommodated him and found the blood bank. He entered the hospital, while we waited in the car. Later in the afternoon he became faint and crashed out in the back of the station wagon. He slept for the rest of the trip.

No matter how large you are two pints of blood in two days is a lot of fluid for the body to make. My oversized travel companion was lucky he was not laid out for a week.

When I gave blood in Athens, I found out my blood type, B-, was fairly rare. The Greek gentleman who bought it for his mother with the same blood type came out to thank me personally. The mother could not have the operation without the blood. The son even gave me his phone number to call when I came back to town. He was ready to buy blood directly from the source, which in this case was me. Wow, I was in demand in Greece and never knew it. I may have saved a life just because I sold blood.

Istanbul, the city most visited by tourist when traveling to Turkey, is not the capital of the country. It is the center of culture and life in Turkey but the government is far away in Ankara. Istanbul is situated at the doorway to the Middle East. This is a city one should visit when traveling to Eastern Europe. Istanbul's slant towards the west is much more evident today than in 1971. The movie, The International, with actor Clive Owens, contained footage of modern Istanbul. I kept telling Scott, the person I saw the movie with, the city streets appeared much cleaner in the movie since my last visit forty years before. The city contains new buildings and public transportation. None of these modern examples were present in 1971.

The Blue Mosque presented in the movie just as magnificent as it did in 1971. This holy place of worship is in the center of Istanbul. It was built between 1609 and 1616 during the reign of Ahmed 1, and remains the architectural wonder of the city. Other mosques exist throughout the Muslim world with the same name. The different mosques carry the blue name because of the blue tiles used to complete the interiors of these wonderful masterpieces. (Blair, Bloom)

While in Istanbul I participated with the culture as much as I could. This enjoyment included food and drink. I went to a teahouse on the Bosphorus Sea and smoked a big wad of tobacco from a hookah. Tea or chai, as it is called in the East, is served with the large pipe and tobacco. As I sat with my chai and smoke, I watched the ferry boats, lit up like Christmas trees, moving up and down the channel of the waters in front of me.

Coffee, another drink in Turkey, is worth trying. It is so thick one could stand a spoon upright in it. A piece of candy is placed in the mouth of a customer first because drinking this black mud straight would be an experience too bitter to enjoy.

Chapter 18
Turkish Puzzle Rings

One of my greatest accomplishments, while in Turkey and Greece, helped the Turks and Greeks bridge an economic trade gap. Turks and Greeks do not like each other. Problems between the two countries extend back hundreds of years when each empire from the two countries kept taking over the other's land. Religion from each country, being different from the other, contributed to the polarization.

The crusades during the medieval period in history did not help. Istanbul is the route most of the crusaders went through on their way to the real fighting in the holy lands. Istanbul became a city of change from one religion to another depending upon who held the military power at the time.

While walking through the Great Bazaar in Istanbul I came across an item dating back to the crusades. The object of this discussion is called Turkish Puzzle Rings. The history of the rings, as told to me by the ring maker, is as follows:

When the knights of the Muslim world went off to war in the holy city of Jerusalem, the rings would find their way onto the fingers of the Turkish wives. The ring would ensure the faithfulness of these women. The rings contain four to eight separate parts interlocked together. When removed from the finger, the ring falls apart. The ring remaining as one piece is only possible if kept on the woman's finger.

If a warrior, returning from battle, found the ring removed from his wives' finger he would assume she had been unfaithful. The woman would then be subject to the severe customs of the society. If the reader thinks women are treated poorly in the Muslim world of today, can you imagine how they were treated hundreds of years ago?

The rings in Turkey existed as the equivalent to the Chastity Belts worn by the wives of the knights from the Christian world. These warriors also had to protect their property when they were doing battle in the holy wars. What I learned about these belts seemed a bit harsh. The belts, worn by the women to prevent intercourse, contained a locking system. The key to this instrument of sex control probably remained in a secret location until the knight's return. Different websites contain pictures of such belts. The design showed the danger of intercourse remained with the man attempting adultery.

Google Chastity Belts and you will see from the pictures which sex was the intended victim. Ouch!

I don't know how you as a reader feels about comparing the two different methods warriors used to keep the fairer sex faithful. I would wager if a vote were taken among women today as to which of the two systems seemed more palatable, the rings would win.

I bought a ring. After a demonstration by the seller, I soon became efficient in putting it back together. Knowing how to return the rings to their original shape must have been valuable information during the middle ages. Those ring makers selling the rings might be offered money to refit the rings to their original place on the fingers of the wives before husbands returned from battle.

The Chastity Belt makers also may have conducted a side business by helping women remove or replace the belts. Information like this is not covered in any of the world history books I've read. This is my theory based on the statement,

"When an opportunity arises, there will always be someone there to fill it."

I became interested in the rings more than any other item found in the bazaar. I discovered the ring factory after asking many sellers working in the countless stalls throughout the market. Upon finding the factory I was shocked as to what I found.

Young boys, between eight and ten years old, made the rings under the supervision of the owner and boss. The boys, with their small fingers, easily cleaned up the rings after they came out of the molding casts. They also took pride in showing me how fast they put the rings back together. The fastest youth could complete the ring in 5 seconds. The same task took me at least one and a half minutes. These boys, if they lived during the Holy Wars, might have become high paid saviors of the wives left behind in Turkey. A good amount of money could be accumulated putting rings back together again.

The rings were made with gold, silver and a third kind of metal. Silver remained at a low price in 1971. I came up with an idea. Other tourists in Europe might be interested in this novel ring. I ordered about 30 rings in different sizes, all made of sterling silver.

I returned to Greece a week later and journeyed to another Greek Island called Naxos. On this island, in the summer of 1971, history unfolded between the nations of Turkey and Greece.

On the beach, I laid out a blanket and displayed the rings. Tourists, who had not traveled to Turkey, knew nothing about the rings. Puzzle rings could not be found in any gift stores in Greece and the fascination around them drew instant sales. With every sale, I needed to show the buyer how to put the rings back together again. This action took time but the sales kept coming and I knew I held a hot item.

After three days of selling these rings, one of the merchants from one of the nearby stores came over to me. He noticed tourists buying these interesting rings. He never knew anything like them existed. Istanbul was not on his list of places he had visited. He did not come over because he held an interest in the rings. He came over to give me a choice. I could either sell all the rings to him at a small profit or continue to sell them on the beach by myself. Choice number two would involve the police because he said I did not possess a license to sell to the tourists. In other words, 'My way or the highway. Sell me the rings or go to jail.'

I discovered during my travels an important rule to follow. When there is a conflict and you are the foreigner, the path of least resistance is the one to take. I sold the rest of the rings to him and headed back to Istanbul. I knew I discovered something valuable and I decided to play my hand and find out where these rings would take me.

When I returned to Turkey, I wanted to visit the coast and beaches along the Mediterranean Sea. I first placed my order for new rings and then picked up an Australian traveler who also showed interest in such a trip. We packed the car and headed south along the coastline.

The first stop contained the site believed to be where the city of Troy once stood. Guides directed tourists to the area where a few ruins remained. After seeing the site, not enough evidence remained to convince me the city of Troy and the famous story surrounding the city ever existed here.

I walked around the grounds for a while trying to find more ruins to indicate the truth behind this site. All of a sudden a Turk came out from behind a tree and beckoned me to follow him. I did so without giving too much thought as to why he wanted me.

Behind a rock stood a wooden part of a horse leg from the hoof up. Standing about two feet high, it was hollow and rustic. The diameter was about eighteen inches with burn mark sections at the top of the leg. I am sure the reader can guess what the Turk was selling.

This leg is what remained from the Trojan horse and I could have it for a mere $75. I wish I possessed the means to send it home. The leg of the famous horse would make a wonderful umbrella holder as well as a fantastic subject of conversation. Alas, the purchase could not be made. I sometimes wonder how many of those famous legs are found by the front doors of other travelers who visited the site of Troy?

The Aussie and I continued south, further along the coast. We found a small town located at the site of a Roman seaside village. My companion heard from other travelers that Roman coins could still be found in the rubble of this site. He was determined to find one.

I hung out on the beach and swam for several hours each day. This dedicated Aussie, instead of relaxing, dug and spread out dirt and trash at the site in hopes of finding a relic. He remained resolute in his quest, much like a bulldog searching for his lost bone.

Guess what? On day four he found his coin. The small black disk, about the size of a dime, portrayed the image of a head on one side. The Aussie expressed so much excitement after his discovery I do not think he slept that night. My friend was offered a sum of money by the local archeologist who worked at this site. No amount of cash was going to separate this Aussie from his coin. He owned a treasure and a lifetime tale as to how he obtained it.

We headed back to Istanbul where we picked up a few more travelers and my order of puzzle rings. The jewelry was ready upon my return. I set out to make a killing in Greece and I possessed the rings to complete the task. With my return to Greece, I was about to make my mark in international relationships.

This time, while in Greece, I went around to the stores in Athens. I showed the rings and demonstrated how they were put together. No one in Athens knew about the rings or even knew they existed. I sold all the rings I owned in just a few days. If anyone wants to check this fact out, here is the truth. Turkish Puzzle rings were not found in Greece before 1971. I became the Marco Polo of Puzzle Rings in Greece.

I returned a year later, after traveling to India, and the Puzzle rings could be found everywhere in Athens. Trade between the Greeks and Turks in the tourist business had jumpstarted. My accomplished deed unfolded with an item dating back to medieval times.

If you ever get to Athens and see these Turkish Puzzle rings in the markets, now you know how they made their journey to Greece. The event happened in 1971 and was accomplished by the guy *'living beneath the radar.'*

Chapter 19
Heading East

When I visited the island of Mykonos, earlier in the summer, I met two brothers working in a restaurant on the beach selling items they brought back from India. I took no interest in the sale items but instead became attracted to the map hanging on a wall behind them. The chart showed India and the surrounding countries of Nepal, Pakistan, Afghanistan and South East Asia. Through the middle of the mentioned countries was a red line extending from Turkey to India.

The brothers traveled across Turkey, Iran, Afghanistan and Pakistan to reach India and Nepal. India is where they stayed for the winter. Both brothers returned to Greece in the summer bringing jewelry and other items to sell. They made enough money in Greece to return to India, live for a year and travel back to the islands. They created a lifestyle involving travel, seeing the world and selling their goods to the youth of the world on a beach in Mykonos.

I knew when I saw the brothers map, this was a trip I wanted to make. I felt a pull I cannot explain. This feeling of adventure and exploring the unknown enveloped my entire being. The meeting of the brothers and my decision to follow their same route through the Middle East became my life changing moment. I would not look back and say to myself,

"What would my life be like if I traveled to India?"

The opportunity to make this journey was now.

Steve remained on the island of Ios. In a letter, he said I should sell the car. He did not share the same desire I held. He wanted to remain in Europe a while longer and return to the states.

I had a few things to do before I headed east. First I had to sell the Opal station wagon and reduce my belongings to what I could carry in a backpack. I held a sale out of the back of the Opal in the parking lot beneath the Parthenon in Athens. Camping gear sold quickly. Within a few days, all the unnecessary goods were sold.

Four young men from Egypt showed up on day four. They showed interest in the car. They came from wealthy families and chose to see Europe while still young. The Opal station wagon suited them just fine.

Selling a car in 1971 simply meant I needed to have the ownership stamp removed from my passport. When a traveler comes into a country in Europe, the border guards places a stamp in the passport showing the owner arrived with a car. The traveler must leave the country with the car or show papers proving the car sold. The stamp also demonstrated to the border guards the correct taxes were paid on the car's sale.

I learned a trick from other travelers in Europe. I could remove the car from my passport by driving to the Yugoslavian border. At the border, I obtained an exit stamp from Greece. At this moment I did not have the car on my passport. I then sell the car in the 200 yd stretch between the two borders. This area is called "No Mans' Land" and is not controlled by either Greece or Yugoslavia. After the car exchange, I return to Greece without the car and without a stamp on my passport. The buyers of the car simply drive into Yugoslavia and allow the car to be stamped into their passports. They now own the car and they are on their way.

The drive to the border took two days. I found the four young Egyptian men a joy to travel with. They sang songs and prayed together the whole journey. This meant pulling over several times along the road in order to meet the required number of prayer times. Praying five times a day is a must if you are a devote Muslim.

The young men shared food and drink with me when we camped out for one night. I am sure their journey into Europe would be as exciting for them as my trip to India would be for me. Experiencing cultures, so different from their own, allowed them to expand their views of the world. I knew my trip to India would do the same and I rejoiced in the idea of the upcoming adventure.

The transfer of the car went smoothly and I returned to Greece. I hitched hiked to Thessaloniki, caught a bus to Turkey, and made travel plans to get to India.

I have a premise. It is not my theory but at the time I did not know about other philosophies sharing speculations regarding the power of the mind. Here is what I discovered on my own. When one sets his or her mind to doing something, the universe gives one the help and directions needed to complete the task. The trick is to take the route of least resistance. This is called "Going with the Flow".

Not until years later would I find a 'New Thought' philosophy using this same theory in their teachings. The mind is a powerful force and can be used to accomplish amazing things.

Chapter 20
Go With the Flow

How does this "Going with the Flow" story sound? I arrived back in Istanbul and stayed at a hotel western travelers used to meet other fellow Europeans and make connections. It was called The Pudding Shop Hotel. I came across a man I knew in college at Santa Barbara. He and another couple owned a VW bus and they needed fellow travelers to share gas expenses all the way to Afghanistan. They departed in a few days and asked if I would like to join them on the trip. An Englishman and German also signed up and would be going with us. The busload of six westerners would be heading east.

I said yes to riding with them. I went to a barber, had my head shaved, exchanged money and said goodbye to Europe and all I held as familiar. I set my mind on a journey to India and the universe gave me a ride all the way to Afghanistan. I went with the flow and did not look back.

Since this all happened in 1971 I do not remember all the names of my fellow travelers except the German. His name was Emil and I remembered him because we traveled together through Nepal and India. I will use the names I believe were the right ones and if any of these people read this book and correct me with their true names, then so be it.

Arthur was an Englishman on the bus. Paul and his girlfriend Pam were the couple who owned the bus. My college friend, Tom, graduated the year before me and I did not have a yearbook with his picture so I could not recheck his name.

On the first day of our travel adventure towards Afghanistan Tom pulled out the 'Lord of the Rings' trilogy for us to read along the way. There were no seats in the back of the bus so each person reading one of the three books in the series could stretch out and read as though they were in a moving living room laying on the floor. Having heard of the books I dove into the adventures, not caring if I was reading them in order or not. Each of the riders in the van read one of the books and then passed it on to another reader when they finished. I can think of no other story ever written that could better parallel what we were doing with the adventure of a few hobbits. Going into the unknown as Frodo and his fellow hobbits did and finding such vast differences in the lifestyles of each new culture we encountered, was indeed a life changing adventure and would alter how we saw the world forever.

We left Istanbul and took the ferry across to Asia where the bulk of Turkey is located. The further east one travels in Turkey the fewer towns and countryside bear any resemblance to Europe. We were entering the Middle East and nothing prepared any of us for what lay ahead. We were all excited and concerned at the same time. Being a bit on edge can be a good thing when traveling because one tends to stay more alert.

The landscape in Turkey is rocky and barren. Except for the occasional flock of sheep crossing the road ahead of the van, there is little to see. Turkey is a rural country. As we headed toward Iran I was reminded of the Moroccan landscape. The main difference between Turkey and North Africa appeared to be the sheep, which replaced the goats. Sheep grazed along the sides of roads and hillsides. Shepherd boys used our van for target practice as we zoomed by but few rocks hit us. Baseball is not played in Turkey. If a rock did hit a windshield of a car or van traveling at 100 km per hour, the damage could be disastrous. I also think some Shepherd boy would get his ass kicked.

We stayed one night in a small town along the route to Iran. Pam, the woman with us, did not feel she needed to adjust to the customs of this Muslim culture. She wore no headscarf and no cover for her bare shoulders.

As we prepared to leave the next morning, a group of village men gathered near our van. They seemed to be in a taunting mood and a few of them attempted to reach out and grab Pam. A single woman traveling with five men in a van while dressed in revealing clothing labeled Pam as a woman of loose morals. With the help of a policeman, who kept the men in line, we climbed into the van and drove out of the village without any real incident.

The point I want to pass on to any other travelers who journey into small remote villages in a country having different values is this. Do not try to impose your culture on them. Make an effort to respect their customs. You are the visitor. Women need to cover their heads, upper arms and legs while traveling in Muslim countries. Do not try and justify your behavior and think you are saving the women from this male dominated society by dressing in revealing clothing. Cover up and be safe. You are not in Kansas anymore.

We were lucky the policeman arrived when he did. If Pam had covered her head and shoulders, nothing would have happened. We were lucky to get out of town without violence.

We drove on towards Iran. Right before the border we could see in the distance the mountain made famous by Noah, Mt. Ararat.

In 1971 Mt. Ararat was believed to be the biblical location where Noah parked the Ark after the great flood. The mountain is also the place where he let all the animals out. The 16,945-foot high mountain is the highest in the region. If you are going to park somewhere it makes sense Mt. Ararat would be the first land seen sticking above the waters. The difficulty would be getting all those animals down the mountain and back to the continents where they belonged. Noah had his hands full.

Chapter 21
Iran

The Shah ruled the country of Iran in 1971. He came to power, with the help of the U.S. government, and he attempted to westernize his country. This process of Iran becoming more like Europe became evident when we reached the capital, Tehran. In Tehran, we could see a real separation in the style of dress worn by the different classes of people.

We stayed in a hotel in the old part of town. Near our hotel women wore the traditional headscarf and long dresses. The men wore clothing typical of other Iranian men throughout most of the country. They wore an outer coat, similar to that worn in the west, but the pants and shirts did not appear as a style I observed in the west. I guess you could call it "native dress".

In 1971 Tehran provided an upper-class section of town where the wealthy government people and their families lived. This part of the population wore clothing styles seen in any European city. Women walked around with uncovered heads. Young men wore the pants and shirts similar to the styles seen in Italy. The boutiques sold all the

Western items one could find in Paris, London or Rome.

The separation of the classes existed in clothing and living conditions. In eight years, without the support of the population, the Shah's term in power came to an end. I am glad I visited Iran before the revolution. I saw some of the conditions existing in Iran, which brought such a drastic change to this part of the world.

As I write this book in 2009, Iran is again poised for another drastic change. Stay tuned. This country, I believe is on the brink of a shift from Muslim fundamentalism to one with closer connections to western ideas and religious openness.

I could see from the videos taken during the election that the clothing of Iran has changed over the years. Western styles appeared on most of the population protesting in the streets. I do not see how fundamentalism can compete with the demands of its' people. The Internet probably is helping the change come about. Populations, living under a religious or military rule, can see how the rest of the world lives. They want the same freedoms existing in open societies.

The stay in Tehran allowed us time to get visas for Afghanistan. Iran makes this task last a few days because they want travelers to spend money in hotels and restaurants. Nothing in the city held our interest as far as things to tour. We did get a chance to eat the food and walk around the bazaars. After three days in town, our visas finally received the needed stamp. We picked them up and headed towards Mashhad, on the border of Afghanistan.

Mashhad is a city, tourist going to Iran should see. A beautiful tomb, dedicated to Khajeh Rabi, is located there. Khajeh, his history not completely clear, lived one of two lives. He possibility accompanied the Prophet Mohammad during his life. Another theory, he lived as a slave or a secretary and companion of Iman Raza, a holy leader of the Shi'ites. The Shi'ites are a sect of the Muslim religion.

The Iman also built a mausoleum in Mashhad dedicated to himself but the tomb of Khajeh Rabi is the mort beautiful of the two. The structure even withstood invasions by the Mogul hordes. The roof of this tomb is inlaid with blue tile and precious stones. I do not know how the inside of the tomb appears because non-Muslim men could not enter. (Iran Chamber Society)

If you are a woman and covered your head, you may tour and view the tomb. These were the rules in 1971. Pam received a scarf for her head, toured the shrine, and came out with the expression of awe and amazement. The men in our group did not appear Muslim. Blond hair and fair skin gave us away.

Mashhad is also known for its' beautiful carpets. Many of the Persian carpets sold around the world come from this city. Mashhad is second in population to Tehran. One day Iran will settle its' disputes with the western world and again tourists from the West can visit these wonders. Mosques and other architecture throughout Persia are a part of the culture and religion. Visit, drink chai, shop for a carpet and visit the Mosque. You will not be disappointed.

Chapter 22
Afghanistan

The border crossing into Afghanistan took us back in time. I wrote about the Medina in Morocco and how a wall divided each town into a new section and an old section. Nothing changed in the Medina for thousands of years. Afghanistan is like one big Medina and there is no new section to go to. This country is how I hoped the Middle East would look like.

The border guards dressed in a type of uniform ever seen by me. The pants and shirt looked like something purchased from the mix and match section at the Dollar Store. Such an appearance made it difficult to respond to the military without laughing. The only way one could tell the men were border guards was this. Each soldier held a rifle resembling a weapon used in WWI. Outdated guns from that war were sent somewhere and I think we discovered which country bought them. The Afghan army used flintlock rifles a hundred years earlier when they held off the British at the Khyber Pass. Now the army carried a weapon with the ability to fire several rounds without reloading.

Herat is the first city you come to when you travel overland from Iran. This community stood out as a town left behind, even for Afghan standards. Mud-walled buildings existed throughout the town because mud was cheap and concrete did not exist in the budget. Camels, still used for transportation of goods, walked through the streets packed with goods destined to travel to the isolated villages surrounding Herat. For a small amount of money, a camel owner would give you a ride around town. We parked the VW bus and checked into our hotel. The first item on our agenda became apparent. A tour of Herat from the back of a camel was in order.

We had to stay one night in Herat. What to eat became a problem. I assumed the naan or bread was safe. Vegetable dishes, I thought, should also be okay to eat. The meat dishes were suspect. If there existed a time in one's life when the thought of becoming a vegetarian arose, 'now' became the time for me.

Emil, our German companion, knew another way to deal with the possibility of picking up some bug or having stomach upset. Starting in Turkey and continuing into Iran and Afghanistan, the first thing he would do was to purchase a bottle of whiskey at a liquor store. Before and after every meal he would take a shot right from the bottle. He remained convinced the alcohol in the hard liquor would kill any parasites lingering in the food. Either the booze or the power of thought worked because he never got sick. He ate meat even when the flesh seemed suspect as to where it came from.

From Heart, the road to Kabul led south through Kandahar, which in 1971 existed as just another town along the main road in Afghanistan. Who would know, 38 years later, this area would be the stronghold of the Taliban who are Muslim extremists. In 1973, on a return trip to this area, I survived a situation from which I developed a theory as to how the Taliban organization got started. I will save the story for a later date.

I do not remember too much about Kandahar. It seemed to be a rest town and an overnight stop between Herat and Kabul. The hotel in Kandahar rated two stars compared to the half star lodging in Herat. I took the usual precautions and ate naan, fruit, and vegetables while Emil drank his way through the Afghan meat cuisine. His stomach must have been lined with lead.

The others in the group also took precautions in their eating habits, especially the Englishman, Arthur. I do not think he had been out of England before and now he found himself traveling in a culture completely different from what he knew back home. He also could not understand how a country of rag-tag soldiers defeated the British. We both later found the answer on the road to India.

Kabul in August placed us in a Muslim capital during the Fast of Ramadan. For the whole month, which is the ninth month of the Muslim calendar, devotes eat and drink nothing from sunrise to sunset. They also abstain from sex and do not smoke during this period. I wonder how well such a holy practice in America would be accepted. Men in the states would become real grumpy and unable to perform such a religious practice. No sex or smoking from sunrise to sunset. The tobacco and condom industries would not allow it. The lobbyists for both these products would be working overtime to stop such a practice.

The Afghan men accept and have practiced this holy observance since they were children and they still get upset. A word of wisdom needs to be passed on to travelers in Afghanistan during Ramadan. Walk softly and do not carry a big stick. If you piss off the Afghan men, they will kick your ass. These are the people who held off the British army from invading their country. They are a tough population of people. When you travel in Afghanistan and observe the environment they live in, one can see why they have to be strong in order to survive.

The capital, Kabul, is also the destination of European and American youth who want to smoke the best hashish in the world. Not only does this country grow poppies for their opium trade, they also make hash for smoking. Black hash could be obtained easily. The drug was used openly in 1971 because it was legal to smoke.

We checked into a famous travelers hotel called Sigis. The hotel became the place to stay while in Kabul in the 70s. I remember the hotel having a giant chessboard on the front patio with pieces about two feet tall. There was always a match going on as well as hash pipes being passed around by the onlookers. The owner, a master chess player, always kept a keen eye open for a worthy challenger to play.

The city of Kabul appeared to be going through a transition in the food industry. Europeans and Americans were coming to this third world country in droves. Items of western food became necessary. Sugar filled foods met those needs.

A baker from the west, traveling through Kabul, saw a need and filled it. I heard the story while waiting in line at the bakery store. A western baker taught a local bread maker how to make junk food most desired by stoned westerners. Donuts, apple turnovers, and jelly filled cakes kept the line of hippies constantly coming. The demand for the above items became so intense, the baker needed to post hours on the door as to when the next batch of sweets came out of the oven. All the sweets sold out within an hour.

I am sure the hotel and bakery no longer remain in operation. The Russian invasion and the Taliban take over of the country probably closed the bakery. Sugar snacks represented a product of western degradation and not good for a Muslim fundamentalist. Look what the overuse of sugar created in America, the most overweight country in the developed world. Where else is there a reality show with contestants, hundreds of pounds above their healthy weight, trying to win a title called 'The Biggest Loser.'

Playing chess is also a western pastime and not a part of the fundamentalist culture after the takeover. The Taliban created another game requiring less thinking and more group participation. During the half-time activities at the main weekend soccer match women are brought out to the center of the field. Stones are involved and I will say no more.

Read the book, 'The Kite Runner', for the details and find out how harshly this fundamental sect of Islam controlled and ran Afghanistan for many years.

Downtown Herat 1971. Camels were the means of transporting supplies at this time.

Chapter 23
Pakistan and India

In Kabul, all the riders in our group went separate ways. Paul, Pam, and Tom sold their VW van, made a good profit and headed off to India and Nepal. The van would be used as a transport vehicle and easily earn back the money paid for it. Third world countries possess a special mechanical gift. They can keep cars and busses going for years and years using skills unknown in the West. I believe duct tape holds many of those vans together today.

Emil, Arthur and I decided to team up for the journey to Nepal. We used public transportation and in third world countries, this means taking a bus. The first leg of the journey took us through the Khyber Pass into Pakistan. At the Khyber Pass I released any doubt I held as to how the Afghanistan rag-tag army held off the British from invading their country. Steep walls exist on both sides of the pass and an army has nowhere to go but forward or backward.

Even though the Afghans only used flintlock rifles, shooting Redcoats in the valley below would be like shooting fish in a barrel. The British were not able to advance into Afghanistan and they eventually gave up. Arthur could not accept this fact. Oh well.

Transportation through the pass stopped when darkness set in. In 1971 bandits controlled the route at night and unless one drove a tank or owned a big gun, no one in their right mind took a chance. Afghanistan remained like the 'wild west' in the early 70s.

Peshawar is the first town we came to after crossing the border into Pakistan. Being a border town, the population was a mixture of three cultures. Afghans, Pakistanis, and Indians. Even today the same mixture of people live in the region.

My first educational moment in Pakistan happened soon after crossing the border. Along with Emil, and Arthur, five Pakistani children surrounded us, wanting to practice their English. They would not let us alone. Just because the British have gone does not mean they have not left their mark. English is still the language used in government and any job requiring a college degree. In India the official language is Hindi but the truth is if you want a top job, you better learn English.

I loved being around inquiring minds. As we continued to swap questions with the children, I finally got to the personal level of conversation by asking their names. I was especially interested in the cute little girl who tied her hair up in a bun on her head with a small cloth cover over the top. She appeared as the only one who wore this hairstyle. After all the boys identified themselves I pointed to the young girl and asked,

"What is her name?"

The face of the girl changed to one of embarrassment as the other boys started to laugh. She then spoke in her native language to her companions and she sounded angry. One of the boys, who spoke the best English, told me,

"He is not a girl."

"Oh" I replied. "Why does he have long hair tied up in a bun?"

"He is a Sikh and he never cuts his hair," was the reply.

I just discovered a new religion. I knew nothing about the Sikhs before I came to Pakistan. The male Sikh wears a turban, grows out his beard and never cuts his hair. Sikhs are the warrior class in India. They are the generals commanding the army, mechanics driving cabs and personal guards protecting the political leaders of India.

In the case of Indira Gandhi, having a Sikh as her personal guard became her biggest mistake. In 1984, Mrs. Gandhi sent troops into the Golden Temple, the holiest shrine for the Sikh religion. Separatists were hiding in the temple. Instead of negotiating or waiting for the rebels to surrender, she decided to show force and a shootout occurred. This military attack on the Temple would be comparable to sending Italian troops into the Vatican and shooting up the place.

The use of force led to the assassination of Indira Gandhi, the Prime Minister of India, by her personal Sikh bodyguard. The guard became a martyr in the eyes of the Sikh population and Mrs. Gandhi became a dead political figure because of her actions.

We next traveled to the capital of Islamabad, which seemed to be in political upheaval. This part of the world was months away from a war with India. The outcome would change the country of East Pakistan into Bangladesh. The conflict would also continue the tensions between India and Pakistan for years to come. I was more than happy to move on to Lahore and finally into India and the city of Amritsar.

Chapter 24
The Sikhs and the Golden Temple

The city of Amritsar is the center for the Sikh Religion. Located in the city is the holy shrine called the Golden Temple. If you ever get a chance to visit the state of Punjab in India you must visit this special place. The central temple, surrounded by a small lake filled with clear blue water, constitutes the place of worship. An outer courtyard surrounds the lake. A walkway guides the worshipers and visitors to the inner temple in the middle of the lake. Special readers are constantly chanting the verses from the Granth. The Shri Guru Granth is a collection of writing of the 6th through the 9th gurus.

A guru is a leader or teacher of religious teachings in India. The first guru and founder of the Sikh religion was Shri Guru Nanak Dev Ji. He lived from 1469 to 1538. Growing up in an area now known as the Punjab, the young Nanak received teachings by the Muslim and Hindu religions. The Sikhs believe they are a part of the Hindu religion and teach "The Brotherhood of Humanity." They feed the poor and needy every day at the Golden Temple as well as in all the Sikh temples throughout the world. The Sikh religion is the fifth largest organized religion. (Gray, Martin)

The warrior-like aspect of the religion developed because of their location between the Muslim and Hindu populations. Sikhs were constantly being attacked by these two religions, trying to convert them to their belief system. Finally, the tenth Guru said,

"Enough!"

This militant stance by the Sikhs happened after the ninth guru lost his head courtesy of a Muslim ruler. The reason for the execution followed the refusal of ninth Guru to convert to Islam. The tenth guru started to train his followers in the skills of being warriors. The Sikhs were ready to kick some butt.

Five aspects of a Sikh male need to be in his possession. He must not cut his hair. He must not cut his beard. A knife called a Kirpan is with him at all times. He must wear a particular type of boxer shorts. An armlet is worn on his wrist. He uses a special comb for his hair. Hair and beard are classified as one item so the list totals five.

Since the tenth guru, the Sikh warriors no longer were caught in the middle of two different religions. The Sikhs learned to stand up for themselves and today they hold the top positions in the Indian military ranks. If you pick on a religious sect too much they will eventually learn how to defend themselves. Israel is a prime example of this fact but right now we are writing about India.

Sikhs are found worldwide. There were a few Sikhs living in Flagstaff when I lived there. These are American converts choosing to become a Sikh and not born as one. I have not seen any of them carrying a Kirpan. It is usually in the steam room or sauna at the gym where we cross paths. There is no need for such an item in a steam room and the metal would get real hot next to your skin.

The one thing no longer permitted in the life of a male Sikh, since 9/11, is the carrying of the Kirpan onto an airplane. Such a weapon would not be allowed. A traveling Sikh would need to check it with his bag or make a special arrangement to keep it in a safe place until the plane arrived at its' destination. The world is changing and everyone is forced to adapt to the restrictions imposed upon us due to the actions of a few radical extremists.

I recently went to a Sikh temple in Glendale, AZ and I asked a few of the Sikh men about the carrying of the Kirpan onto a plane. They acknowledge the changes and said they put the knife through with checked bags. Sikhs understand the world has changed for them as well as everyone else and adaptation is necessary.

Chapter 25
Nepal and the Himalayas

Emil, Arthur and I traveled across northern India and took a left heading north towards Nepal and Katmandu. I held one major goal since my meeting with the two brothers selling Indian items on the beach in Greece. Trekking in Nepal. One brother told me about the hike towards Mt. Everest. I remained focused on the journey and accomplishing the trek while I still could.

The month of October arrived in Nepal. By talking to many of the westerners living in Kathmandu that fall is one of the best times to trek in the Himalayan Mountains. The dry season lasted until winter and the snows didn't arrive until December or January. By then the passes would be difficult to cross and the cold weather would make the experience unpleasant.

The group of travelers including Arthur, Emil, Paul, Pam and Tom all said our final goodbyes in Katmandu after we all met again in Nepal. Only Emil and I prepared to stay and trek in Nepal. Paul and Pam were no longer an item by the time they reached Nepal. She seemed angry with Paul and he as well with her. I wonder how their trip from Kabul to Katmandu went? Not too good it seemed.

Paul needed to return to the states and find out if he passed the Bar exam. Tom needed to find work in a law firm since he passed the Bar just before leaving the States. Pam desired to find another boyfriend and she let us know, regarding her availability. A woman alone in an eastern country might feel vulnerable. Male or female companionship could help in this matter.

Arthur expressed little interest in seeing the Himalayan Mountains. My love for the difference the East presented did not jell with Arthur. He constantly compared England with India. He hated everything around him and he ended each day with a new list of complaints. He probably felt disconnected in a country, which spoke English but produced nothing reminding him of his homeland.

When last seen Arthur and some other English travelers connected and combined their lists of reasons why one should hate India. Thank God the sun did set on the British Empire. The English must have been hard to live with while they controlled most of the world in the 19th century.

Emil expressed interested in doing the Everest trek. He didn't have to be back to Alaska until January where he worked on the oil pipeline as a welder. He earned a large salary because he worked on the Alaska project in the winter months. Emil seemed to be a person who could do anything in tough weather conditions. His build reminded me of a running back football player. He may have been short but he exuded power in all aspects of his body.

Emil, a product of the European education system, possessed welding skills since the age of 17. He now traveled the world during his time off.

The first thing you have to do, when you go trekking or mountain climbing in the Himalayan Mountains, is to get a permit. The country of Nepal contained a natural wonder. The highest mountains in the world made up the backbone of the country and a fee to climb and trek produced income.

A few days would be needed for my trekking permit to clear government bureaucracy. Little is accomplished quickly in the east, especially paperwork. During the wait time, I tried to get in climbing shape and break in my almost new hiking boots purchased in Switzerland.

A certain temple in Katmandu presented some very steep steps climbing straight up a hill. I received some advice from another western trekker. I should go up and down these slabs of stone four times each day until I left on the hike. This exercise would help get me in shape. I made it up and down twice. The next day I could hardly move. I was in trouble.

Emil obtained his permit the day before I did. He decided to start the trek right away. He needed to get back to Alaska. I followed the next day and we agreed to meet in Namche Bazaar, a Sherpa village near the end of the trek. The town, located on the way to the base camp of Mt. Everest, could not be missed. The trek is 300 miles long or 150 miles each way. The journey is 10 to 12 days to Namche Bazaar. It took me 11 days.

The first part of the trip included a bus ride from Katmandu to the trailhead. Hikers need a map to know which village one would be walking to each day. The map marked the villages at ten to twelve miles apart.

Merchandise needed in the small villages along the route is carried in on the backs of coolies. Coolies are paid Nepalese transport workers. They each pack a cone shaped basket on their backs with a strap across their foreheads. The weight of these baskets is anywhere between 75 to 150 pounds. Young boys start learning how to do this job with 50 pounds on their shoulders.

What I noticed about these short Nepalese coolies pertained to the size of their legs and calves. Never before have I seen such muscular legs in proportion to the size of the body. Their legs, accompanied by bare feet, showed a people who were tough as well as strong.

Shoes remained a luxury to these transporters of goods. The hard, leathery soles of the feet of a Nepalese man indicated their occupation. These coolies were so strong, I could not keep up with their pace on the trail. I was carrying 25 pounds and they were carrying 100 to 150 pounds.

I arrived at the trailhead around noon and started hiking straight up the mountain. No easy flat section existed to warm up and stretch. I arrived at the first teahouse, on the route, around five in the afternoon. I worried that death finally caught up with me.

The new boots on my feet were not broken in. In 1971, hiking boots weighed about two or three pounds each. The boots today weigh about half a pound together. My heels bled, my legs throbbed and every other part of my body felt only pain.

In a teahouse, there is a small fee for sleeping on the floor. There is another charge for a big plate of rice and locally grown vegetables. I managed to eat about half the serving of dinner. Afterwards, I went right to bed. Day one accomplished with ten more to go.

The next few days of walking seemed a blur. I remember having to dress my bleeding heals each morning and evening. My muscles eventually adjusted to the miles of pounding they took each day. I know now that at age 26 this trek was possible. Today, at age 64, there is no 'friggen' way I could make this trip. I made the right choice when to do the trek. I am grateful to be able to do this once in a lifetime adventure.

Most of the trek is up and down the foothills of the Himalayan. The foothills reach 12,000 feet in elevation. You also traverse valleys containing villages surrounded by fields of crops. These small communities are isolated and produce much of their own food to survive.

During the day, a view of the Himalayan Mountains to the north usually is possible. While in the valleys, the peaks are hidden temporally. There are few places in the world where a trekker can see such high peaks while on the trail. Peru is the other locale in the world and the Andes are another such mountain range.

By the fifth day, my body started to adjust to the physical beating and my heels stopped bleeding. My head cleared and I became more in the moment. I could now enjoy my surroundings and take in the beauty of Nepal.

On day six I still remained alone and trekked by myself. In the afternoon I witnessed something few tourists ever see. Walking along the trail towards me came three men dressed in animal skins and carrying pitchforks. Each one wore paint markings on their foreheads. Their hair appeared as if it had never been cut. The long strands somehow were arranged in a twisted pile on top of their heads. I had not been in India long so I did not know who or what I was seeing. When they passed me I felt an energy field travel through my body. The men each gave me an intense stare as they passed. I am sure I seemed as much of a novelty to them as they were to me.

I found out later, after describing these men to other travelers when I returned to Katmandu, they were Lord Shiva Sadhus. The probability of crossing their path might have been sheer luck. Sadhus tend to live isolated and private lives. One suggestion, coming from another westerner, made sense. The holy men were moving to a low elevations before winter arrived.

One of the men appeared much older and his white hair confirmed fact. The two younger men may have been training under the older ascetic. Sadhus go high up into the Himalayan Mountains away from any population. They practice meditation and other forms of physical and mental training.

The path of a Shiva disciple brings the followers closer to God, Brahma, Shiva, Allah or any other name given to this higher power. Sadhus are viewed by many western religions as the crazy people of the Hindu religion. Because God is called by a different name in different religions, we fight holy wars. Who are the real crazies?

By day seven I felt in the groove. The miles were flying by as I walked. My body became a fat burning machine and my muscles responded well and ceased being in constant agony. At night I could eat two of those large plates of rice and vegetables and maybe a cookie for dessert. I could pack the food in and my body would use the calories just as fast the following day.

At noon on day seven, I approached a village preparing a special festival meal. The elders of the village spoke fairly good English. They invited me to share in the feast for the whole community. Large quantities of rice and other foods simmered over the fires while the cooks gave the final spice touches to each dish.

This village was a Nepalese Hindu community and because of the location far from any major city or town, the practice of the caste system still existed. Observing who did all the work, I thought the advantage for this meal went to the lower caste population. The Brahmans or higher caste men did all the cooking.

Because the lower cast cannot touch the food or clothing of the upper caste, the Brahman men cooked and washed dishes for the entire community. When the time came for the food to be eaten, large quantities of rice and vegetables needed to be passed onto the lower castes of the town. To accomplish the moving of food and still abide by the no- touch law, the rice and later the vegetables were launched into the air out of the Brahman's food basket. Waiting for the meal five feet away, the lower caste held out their basket and caught the items for lunch before anything touched the ground. The passing of the food took time but eventually everyone received the Brahman cooked, air-dried meal.

I do not think this approach to cooking will work if Macdonald's or Burger King ever opens up in this village. The Brahmans would do all the cooking and, because of the caste system, throw the burgers out of the pickup windows to the members of lower castes. French fries might get a little messy. Malts and shakes also would need a special sealed cup or people would be wearing lunch instead of eating it. Let's hope this never happens.

As I sat among the village elders I sensed a reason for my invitation to the ceremony. In the East, nothing happens without a reason. For the village Brahmans, my arrival was auspicious. The elders believed I arrived at their village on this special ceremonial lunch day to become the English teacher for their children.

The leaders asked me about my educational background. They smiled upon discovering I received a college education. Some English primers appeared out of nowhere and I read to a few of the young male boys sitting with us at lunch.

For a man to get a good job in Nepal, especially in government, English needed to be learned in school and the study of the language became a top priority. These young children required fluency in order to obtain work in Kathmandu.

I became confused and torn between my two choices. I could stay in this village in the middle of the Nepalese countryside and teach English, or continue my trek to Namche Bazaar. I told the elders I would continue my trek. I said I would think about a decision and give them an answer on my return.

The look on their faces told me they needed an answer now. They would not wait for my auspicious decision. My leaving to them meant I was not interested. Not until my return trip, a week later, did I realize they knew the truth. I was not prepared to be isolated from civilization. This village remained seven days walk from the bus, which took one into Kathmandu, and three days walk to the nearest airport. This teaching job existed outside of my comfort zone.

I stayed the night in a hut provided for me and continued on my way in the morning. I felt overwhelmed by the experience of the day before. I wanted to finish the hike. Completing the trek became a personal challenge and any diversion needed to wait.

Whoever took the teaching job in the village would be able to write a whole novel regarding the experience. If anyone reading this book knows the person who taught English to Nepalese boys in the middle of the countryside, let me know. I would love to hear from you.

A wooden pot maker carves a vessel using the stream to turn the lathe wheel as he carves.

For the last two days on the trek I traveled with a young man from New York. He left Kathmandu the day after me but caught up when I stayed at the village during the festival. He approached the trek with an unusual angle. Every time he came to a hill he pulled out some cocaine, snorted a line, and sped his way up and over the pass.

I never tried cocaine before. The one time I did experience it with him I did not feel much from the effect. By now I was in good hiking shape and I really didn't need cocaine to get me over a hill. We parted ways when we reached the Sherpa village of Namche Bazar. He took a detour to the airport because he chose to fly back. He probably ran out of cocaine and didn't think he could manage a return trip under his own power.

As I approach the village of Namche I received a greeting by 50 half-naked children. The tribe came screaming and running down the hill towards me. I assumed they used such an approach with every new hiker coming to their village. Running towards a stranger seemed to be their way of having fun.

The village of Namche Bazar, 1971

I decided to give them a return gift. I raised my arms in the air and started yelling and running straight at them just to see how they would react. The ones closest to the front of the pack portrayed the look of pure panic on their faces and jumped to the side.

The mob parted like the Red Sea when Moses escaped from Egypt. When I ran past them the older boys saw me laughing and they knew I was only kidding. They returned to their initial intent. Scare the tourist and beg some money. It was too late. I managed to scramble up the hill and into the village. I rented a room and knew I was now safe from the Nepalese version of 'Lord of the Flies'.

I finished what I set out to do. I made the trek to Namche Bazar. I set my goal and through pain and discomfort, the final objective was accomplished. The halfway point of the Trek may not be like mile 13 of the Boston Marathon but I bet the internal accomplishment felt pretty close.

Namche Bazar is located in the Khumbu region of Nepal. The lowest elevation of this hillside village is 11,286 feet. I think where I slept in town seemed about 500 feet higher. The peaks surrounding Namche rise to elevations topping 20,000 feet and remain snow-capped all year.

Strange looking yak cows roam the fields and pathways. These are yaks bred with low elevation cows. This enables the high elevation population to get good milk production. The yak cow wears the fur coat of a full-blooded yak and sports the milk utters of a lowland cow. In other words, warm milk on the hoof.

The Sherpa population comes from Tibetans having moved into Nepal years before Nepal became a country. Most of their villages are at high elevations just like the villages of their homeland. Tibetan Buddhism is their religion. The men and women are the guides leading European and American groups up the majestic peaks surrounding Namche.

Sherpas are paid well. After observing the quality clothing and expensive watches the Sherpa men and women wear, the industry of mountain climbing still seems to be thriving.

A charge or fee exists for climbing anything above 15,000 feet in Nepal. Government people are posted along the routes to these mountains. Such a government building existed in Namche. I crossed the village hillside to the government post to check in with my trekking permit and receive a stamp showing I arrived at the destination. The government post is also a safety check to make sure no hikers wandered off into the wilderness of Nepal. A wrong turn could take a trekker into Bhutan or back to India.

Chapter 26
Six Years in a Cave

During the three days I remained in Namche a special celebration took place in the small Tibetan Temple located in the village. The innkeeper spoke English and told me about the event. In the Tibetan tradition, special meditation retreats exist in which a monk or nun can complete but they require a bit of time and dedication. A six-year course or the longer twelve-year retreat is available depending on one's busy schedule.

A nun had completed the shorter six-year meditation retreat and a few high Lamas or Tibetan holy men gathered at the temple to chant, drink Tibetan tea and honor her accomplishment. The Tibetan cymbals, horns and singing of the verses filled the airways surrounding the temple.

This is how the event is accomplished. The person wanting to perform such an in-depth contemplation is sealed in a cave. There is a stream flowing through the cavern, which takes care of washing and bathroom needs. I did not ask too many questions about this last duty.

Food is prepared by monks outside the chamber and passed into the cave through a slot in the doorway. The monks on the outside take care of all the nourishment needs of the meditating Nun. The hole in the door is then resealed. The Nun is in total darkness during the time she spends in contemplation. When the retreat is completed, as in the case of the Nun, celebration occurs.

On one of the nights of chanting I ventured over to the temple with three other hikers to watch the monks. We were greeted with smiles, given tea to drink and allowed to stay as long as we wanted. The retreat Nun was not in the temple. She probably needed more time to adjust to being around people. I did not give the ceremony much more thought and after an hour of being with the monks we left for the comfort of our beds.

The next day, as I returned to my hotel room after a walk around the hillside, I noticed someone approaching me. From a distance, I could tell the meditating Nun was coming my way. As she drew nearer I noticed every detail of her physical being. The hair remained uncut for six years and the length forced the Nun to tie the dreadlocks into a large knot secured at the waist. Letting the hair down meant dragging locks on the ground. Brushing and combing one's hair, during such a religious practice, holds a low priority.

Her face gave no real indicators of age. My guess placed her around 40. Her skin looked smooth and brown and she wore a big smile covering most of the area below her nose.

When the Nun walked past she looked in me, not at me. I felt a wave of energy permeate my body much like the occurrence with the three Sadhus several days before. I almost fell over from the power force field. The energy vibrated within. At this moment I felt the woman could see all of my past lives as well as the one unfolding in the present. I almost lost my ability to breath.

Had I not been overwhelmed by her force field I might have asked her about my life as a boy on a farm outside Florence, Italy. The Nun probably did not speak English and the Innkeeper who did, could not be found. That moment remained the only time I saw the retreat nun.

After all these years I still remember our meeting as one of the most unforgettable moments in my life. I even carried my camera at the time but did not feel the need to intrude into her personal space by asking for a picture.

Chapter 27
The Top of the World

**The author at Tymboche with Mt. Everest
in the background.**

Later in the day, I hiked up to the next community, two hours away. The small village called Tymboche served as a Tibetan monastery with homes for the monks and rooms for trekking tourists like myself. The hike climbed only a thousand feet in elevation. This proved to be the most difficult walk on the trip. The trouble seemed to center around the elevation. At 13,000 feet I seemed to have hit a wall. I could hardly breathe. I thought I could run up the hill but this proved not to be the case.

I read later about elevation problems hikers tend to encounter. At 13,000 feet and higher, tourists and non-trained climbers can get altitude sickness and become disoriented, sick and uncomfortable. The cause of the sickness is due to lower air pressure at higher elevation, not the lack of oxygen. The reason for base camps and the higher elevation stops set up by climbers is for the men and women attempting the ascent to adjusting to the drop in air pressure.

Tymboche is located in a valley with a gradual climb up to the 16,000 ft. base camp for Everest. I could see the top of Everest sticking out behind some lower peaks from where I stood in Tymboche. To see such an amazing sight should be included in the '100 things to do before you die' list. A 29,000 ft., a mountain towering over smaller 20,000 ft. peaks is a sight indeed. The smaller peaks are the average height of all the mountains in the Andes Mountains in Peru.

For all you travelers who can afford such a trip but not be able to make the trek, there is hope for you. Hotels with airports in nearby valleys exist. One can fly into the valley, check into the hotel and see the peaks from your hotel window. The lodges maintain pressurized rooms with oxygen inside. The experience would be like flying in an airplane except you would be at an elevation of 14,000 ft. and not 35,000 ft. As Nike says, 'just do it.' You will thank me later. The Japanese were building such a hotel in 1971 but it was not completed for tourists to use. I am sure it is available today.

Tymboche is the Buddhist monastery located above Namche Bazaar, 13,000 ft. in elevation.

Emil showed up in Tymboche later in the evening. He just returned from further up the valley where he stayed in a tin shack set up for hikers at about 15,000 ft. in elevation. He spent the night alone. Sitting around the fire in our sleeping dorm, Emil told us of his night on the mountain.

"After I went to bed something large got on the roof of the shack and tried to get in. I locked the door from the inside before going to sleep. I am sure it was the Yeti. I hardly slept all night."

Emil is a brave person who did not seem to get upset about many things. He really showed his emotions telling us his story and fear is what he projected. I bet Emil finished his bottle of whiskey just to get through the night while in the hut by himself.

Two other Americans joined us for our remaining days at this high elevation monastery. One of the hikers told us of another such monastery on the Chinese-Tibetan side of Everest around 19,000 ft. in elevation. I tried to imagine workers building a monastery as well as monks living at such a high elevation. Their lung capacity must be enormous due to the lack of oxygen. No wonder Sherpas and Tibetans born at these heights are the guides taking climbers to the summit of the surrounding peaks.

The next day the four of us headed back to Kathmandu on the same trail we hiked before to get us here. I remain thankful to this day for doing most of the trek by myself. The experiences on the inbound trek with Sadhus and the special village ceremony were mine. As I reflect upon them I felt blessed to be given a gift of those events and I feel passing these stories on to the reader is my gift back to the world.

As I traveled with these other hikers on the return all interactions with the locals changed. One hiker was an 'Ugly American' doctor who treated the Nepalese like his servants. His partner seemed not as aggressive but he still behaved like the doctor towards the locals trying to duplicate his behavior. I can imagine the 'bedside manner' of this practitioner when he helped his patients back in the states. I think the best way for him to practice medicine is to become the doctor who put patients asleep. In such a discipline he does not have to have much interaction with them and they do not need to talk with him. He can keep his God complex to himself and live happily ever after.

Emil on the right and two other hikers on our Trek back to Kathmandu from the Everest.

On the trek back we saw Sir Edmund Hillary from a distance. For the reader who may not know Sir Edmund, he and the Sherpa guide, Tenzing Norgay, were the first men to have climbed Mt. Everest. Sir Edmund happened to be visiting a village below the trail where we walked. He was meeting Nepalese and Tibetan admirers in the courtyard of someone's house. Hillary, when he was alive, spent time and money helping the Sherpas to start schools and raise their standing in society.

We did not try to go down and meet Sir Edmund. What would you say to the most famous mountain climber in the world?

"Jolly good job mate. Way to climb that mountain."

By the time we returned to Kathmandu my knees were wrapped with ace bandages for support. They were extremely sore when I walked downhill. The shock of using my legs to slow my body going downhill placed great stress on the knee joints.

I felt like celebrating upon my return from this once in a lifetime trek. In America, the habit of eating seems to be a part of most celebrations. Emil and I decided to eat.

Our bodies worked like tuned machines upon our arrival into town. I lost 20 lbs. and possessed no fat what so ever. Both of us were gone for twenty-five days. Our diet of rice and vegetables, with an occasional egg and cookie, turned us into hiking powerhouses. Our metabolisms still ran at a high level and demanded food.

In Kathmandu, the western diet replaced the simple food of Nepal in all of the restaurants. Burgers, pies, cakes and other items, not found in the countryside of Nepal now lay within our reach. We spent two days walking around town eating large amounts of this junk food and washing the meal down with a Bong Lassie. A Bong Lassie is a milkshake made from the juice of squished marijuana leaves.

On day three Emil and I woke up sick as dogs. We stayed in bed for 24 hours while our bodies passed all the toxins we inhaled during the previous 48 hours. Bodies are interesting organisms. If you treat them with respect they keep you going and serve you well. Feed them high fat and sugar and they either shut down or you wear the results in weight.

Go trekking in Nepal if you are able. The Golden Arches won't be in the countryside for a long time and you'll become a lot healthier. Just remember not to go on a food binge once back in Kathmandu. Your body will let you know when you have over done it.

The author hanging from bridge on Everest Trek

Chapter 28
Back to India

After a week back in Kathmandu, Emil and I attended a Thanksgiving party full of other American travelers. The Trek changed me and I felt different being around westerners again. The shift came from my having seen and accomplished something many at the party never will. I could not get into the small talk. I came to the east to explore, learn and expand my knowledge of the world. The tourists at the Thanksgiving gathering came to party, drink and talk about how things are back in the states. I seem to be on a completely different journey.

The next day Emil and I headed to Calcutta, India where we planned to fly to Burma and eventually down through South East Asia. I planned to travel with Emil and possibly be back in the States by 1972, or so I thought.

The Indian-Pakistan War changed my plans. The conflict started while trekking in Nepal. While in the middle of the country we received no contact with the outside world. By the time we reached the Calcutta airport a blackout on all flights stopped us in our tracks.

Calcutta is located on the East coast of India near the East Pakistan border. The war seemed to center around the mistreatment of Hindus in East Pakistan. A stream of refugees poured out of the country every day and India decided to do something about it.

Emil traveled with a schedule in which he was obligated to meet. He needed to be back in Alaska in a few months. I didn't. I decided to change direction, stay in India and experience the culture and its' mysteries. I became enchanted by this immense country of 450 million people (in 1971) and up to this moment I had barely touched its' surface.

Emil and I both took the train across the country to Bombay two and a half days away. From Bombay Emil would fly to South East Asia, travel to Australia and return to Alaska in time for the winter shift. We parted ways at the hotel where we stayed in Bombay. Emil seemed to understand how to go with the flow while traveling. He adapted to changing his plans and kept on trekking. Wherever you are Emil if you ever read this thank you for the adventures we shared. If I ever take up drinking whiskey I will always think of you.

I decided to head south to the state of Goa and sit out the war. I heard from other travelers about the beautiful beaches and warm eighty-degree weather. The descriptions painted a wonderful place to be for a while. As I continued moving through India I asked other travelers about great places to visit. Questioning others became my best source to find out information. I did not need to plan out a schedule. I did not have to be back in the states for a job. At this time in my life I could choose any path to travel. Looking back to this moment I do not remember ever standing in a space of unlimited possibilities ever again. It felt free and at the same time overwhelmed.

Chapter 29
Goa

The state of Goa is the smallest of all the states in India. Located south of the state of Maharashtra and situated on the Arabian Sea makes it a perfect place to spend the winter. In the sixteenth century, Portuguese merchants came to Goa to trade. They soon realized the potential of making the area a colony so Portugal conquered Goa and remained for 450 years until 1961. (History of Goa)

In 1961 India annexed Goa with little fanfare. The capital is Panaji and the religion remains Catholic, a legacy of the Portuguese.   The locals still speak Portuguese or at least something resembling the language. Fishing, farming, and tourism are the main industry.

The train to Goa left in the evening from Bombay. Mumbai is now the name for this Indian metropolis but in November of 1971, it was still named Bombay. While in the train station waiting to leave an air raid siren went off and a total blackout took place. Indians took this war seriously. If anyone even lit a match they got blasted with verbal attacks from hundreds of people waiting for the train. Even the Taj Mahal received a cover with dark blankets so the Pakistan air force could not use the white reflection as a landmark during the full moon.

The next morning the train arrived in Goa. I and many other westerners traveling in India came to this beach state to wait out winter. The temperatures from December to February range from 68 as a low and 84 as a high. Beautiful beaches with coconut palms line the coast. Reasonably priced rooms in homes or apartments made the stay in Goa financially feasible for those with limited funds.

I met three Swedish travelers on the train from Bombay. The single Swede named Hans and the couple, Ammi, and Hakan, seemed friendly. We decided to get a place together in Goa. We rented a covered porch area off a fisherman's house right on the beach. We bought kerosene stoves, grass pads for protection under sleeping bags, plates, and silverware. We could either buy fish from the fishermen bringing in a catch every day or get free fish if we helped pull in the nets. We swam daily in the warm waters of the Arabian Sea and sometimes went into the nearby town to enjoy the local cuisine. We were on a vacation like no other we would experience again in our lives.

On Christmas Eve a few westerners and I attended the nearby church, which held a Catholic Portuguese midnight mass. The fishermen and their families arrived at the service dressed in their finest clothing. The shift from seeing them in their daily dress, to the church attire was dramatic. I assumed the beautiful dresses are kept in a special closet along with the suits of the men and brought out only for such events. Goa is the only state in India containing a Catholic majority and the locals took the ceremonial aspects of the religion seriously.

The population of Goa does not look like the people of other parts of India. The mixture of Portuguese and native population for 450 years is the reason for the sharply chiseled features of these inhabitants. The language spoken among the families differed from the Hindi spoken throughout India. I do not speak Portuguese so I could not tell if any of the vocabulary used in the conversations was of European descent.

Farming provided the other foods needed to compliment a fish dinner. If you didn't live near the sea you probably farmed and sold the products produced. Indian business shops could be found in town and most of the products available throughout India were available to the residents of Goa.

During my stay on Colva Beach in Goa, someone told me about a westerner living nearby who brought a surfboard to India. The person said he saw the surfer and his board the day before while at the beach. I happened to be bodysurfing when he told me about the man. The waves were about three feet high and I hoped the board surfer would show up again. He never showed up at the beach and I felt disappointed.

I lost my North African trade bead necklace on this day. The leather string snapped and they came off my neck while in the ocean. I loved those beads. They held good memories of Morocco. There is always a lesson regarding attachment in life. Today I learned to let my necklace go. As I mentioned before in the book, if the beads ever washed up on the shore, the local anthropologists should stay busy figuring out how North African trade beads made their way to India.

I met the board surfer a few days later and found out he came from San Diego like myself. He went to a high school near La Jolla called Kearney High. Someone from near my hometown all the way over here in India with a surfboard. What are the odds?

His name was Don and he was traveling with his girlfriend, Katie, also from San Diego. We swapped surfing stories and asked if we knew so and so and soon kindled a friendship based on similar high school experiences. As far as I know Don is the first westerner to bring a surfboard to India and surf the waves with it.

Life in this Indian beach state remained easy and relaxed. We could get information about the Indian-Pakistan war if we wanted to read a paper but most of us from the West took little interest in the political struggles between these two nations. By February the war ended. Eastern countries in 1972 lacked the funds to continue fighting and this helped bring conflicts to a close. What a way to end a war.

"Sorry, we ran out of money. The war is over. We will only continue the battle if we vote in more funds."

East Pakistan became Bangladesh and the rest is history. The real downside of the war can be seen in the disagreements these two countries maintain today. So far India and Pakistan have stopped short from going over the edge. Both countries have nuclear weapons. Over the edge happens when nuclear countries go too far. The United States remains the only country that went too far and used nuclear weapons on another country.

While staying in Goa I met young people from all over the world. The Swedish and other Scandinavian countries were well represented. There also existed a group of Americans who traveled to Goa together from the States. Robert was one of the young men in that group and he visited me a lot during the Colva beach stay. There is always something connecting people with their nationalities and commonality of growing up. Robert came from somewhere in the midwest like Ohio and I believe he really wanted to live on a beach in California. The sands of Goa were close enough to the west coast experience.

India also attracts people who may have a difficult time living in the west because of their personality not fitting in with the norm of western nations. One such person from Ireland named Ian (made up name due to my lack of memory after 40 years) also lived on Colva beach in Goa. Ireland was a part of the British Commonwealth and Ian could stay in India as long as he wanted to. I heard he had been in Goa for several years and the locals seemed to know about him and his non-orthodox behavior.

To best describe Ian I would have to refer to one of the patients from the movie, 'One Flew Over the Cuckoo's Nest' by Ken Kesey. Some mental patients who do not take their medications lose the ability to use the filters in their brains to screen what they see in people and monitor what comes out of their mouth. When Ian met people he became a non-stop verbal critic of each and everyone he met. He ripped them with a wave of abuse sending the recipient into retreat mode.

During the few times I crossed paths with Ian I learned to not engage in conversation with him. To do so meant suffering the consequences of his verbal onslaught. My American friend, Robert, was not so lucky. One morning the Americans, who traveled to India with Robert, came by our porch on the beach. They told me a story of how, the day before, all of them took LSD and walked around the beach, taking in the beauty of Goa from a different perspective. While on their trip Ian crossed paths with the group and began his verbal, non-filtered insight as to what was wrong with them and what they could do to live life as free (or crazy) as he did.

For some reason, Robert separated from his friends and stayed with Ian for the duration of the LSD trip.

After the hallucinogenic drug wore off Robert became a disciple of Ian and told his American friends he was going to stay in India and spread the wisdom of his new spiritual teacher. Robert's friends were on the lookout for him and told me to please let them know if he came by.

During the next few weeks Robert would appear, sometime with Ian and sometimes alone. He carried a journal of poems and writings and I even allowed him to write in my travel book. Here is one.

Sunshiny Day
by Robert

Sunshine sings in my windowpane-- Let it rain,
Fire warms me now cause there's a piece of me in my
mind, says
Let the Sunshine sing today
O along your lonely way.

Smiled at the sea---said
Be rolling on my way----
Sing this simple song---In some kinda sunshine day.

Now I see a sea of going drowsy waves freezing in a
Blessing Day,
But sunshine, she came with the pay.

Sunshine knows there's gonna be one more day to let my
merry song
Slip gently over your way.

Your way's yellow, my way's grey.
Let there be sunshine today.

Well, the water she rose to sea,
Tripping on sunshine today.
Know my way's slow but can it grow
Before sunshine goes so low.

But sun she's up
And let it see the sunshine singing,
please, fill up my cup.

Touch my eyes,
Feel my mind and sing me
Somekinda sunshine song.

Please go by again
With the line of
My sunshiny song
And Come Back fore Long.

I felt the need to add one of the three entries Robert placed in my journal. There seemed to be a quality of Allen Ginsberg in my spaced out American friend as well as in his physical features. He is in the photo on the bottom left which appears at the end of this chapter.

Robert's friends from the states continued to worry about him and decided to carry out a plan to get Robert home. A few days before I left Goa the story of how the group got Robert back to the states was told. The Americans were able to persuade our Ginsberg poet to take a side trip back to Bombay for some shopping and sightseeing. While in the city, they got him onto a plane at the airport and kidnapped him back to the states. They were afraid he would be another causality in India like Ian the Irishman. I did not get an address for Robert so I never found out if he recovered.

There is a lesson here. When trying out mind-expanding drugs, do not hang out with people who may be living in a different reality. LSD might cause you to see the other side as one you can relate to and the tripper may want to stay there. Mind expansion through LSD is a powerful way to see the world differently. The leap towards different perceptions, all at once, may be too much.

Dr. Richard Alpert, who later became Baba Ram Dass, started out using LSD before seeking a Spiritual life through meditation and contemplation. He went to India and became involved with an Indian Guru named Neem Karoli Baba who became his teacher. Ram Dass is most famous for his book, "Be Here Now". He still travels and lectures, even after a stroke in 1997. He guides seekers to practice meditation. The eastern practice is a means of changing one's self by taking gradual steps. LSD opens up a person suddenly and users may not be ready to make the leap in one bound.

This is the house where I lived in Goa. I am seated in the middle with Hans and Robert to my right. Hakan and Ammi are to my left and Don is standing with the Goan fisherman and his wife.

Chapter 30
Southern India

Winter came to a close in India during the month of March with the temperatures starting to rise. Soon it would be too hot to travel and see the south part of the country. I wanted to travel to the southern end of India so I planned out my trip.

My months in Goa renewed my body after trekking in Nepal. I regained some weight and my energy seemed to be working at a normal level. I found my stay in Goa to be one of revival and connection with new travel companions.

In India, animals are washed and treated with loving care.

My Swedish friend, Hans, with whom I lived in Goa, joined me and we headed down to the state of Kerala by train. Kerala is the only socialist state in India. The period in during which we arrived happened to be the state elections. I have never seen such a passionate population taking part in demonstrations and campaigning. After departing from the train we made our way through the rallies and marches and took a bus to the coast.

We arrived at the seaside village of Kannur. Hans stayed only one night. He experienced enough of the beaches in India. He wanted to head north to Nepal and cooler weather. Heat is something Scandinavians do not appear to favor in large amounts. Hans needed to cool off.

The next day Don, Katie, and his surfboard arrived in Kannur beach. We both grew up near the ocean. We looked forward to being the first to surf some of the wave breaks along the Indian coast. Neither of us knew if sharks or other such meat eating fish swam these same waters. Not until recently did I learn saltwater crocodiles could be found in the oceans and rivers of India. Sometimes ignorance is bliss and in our case I found this fact to be true.

Don's surfboard stood only 5 feet 10 inches long. It represented what surfing had transitioned to since my long board days. The short board responded quickly to the turns of a surfer. The technique in riding such a fast acting wave rider required practice and patience. Most of the boards I surfed were 9 feet or longer. I slowly adapted and soon my short, three-second rides extended into ten or fifteen seconds.

We all enjoyed the beach combing experience for a week. Becoming restless we decided to travel to the southernmost tip of India. At the southern tip is a place called Cape Comorin in the state of Tamil Nadu. We planned the trip so our arrival would be on the full moon. Another friend from Goa joined us. We packed our bags and set off to town to catch the best form of transportation left behind by the British. The train.

Moon cycles are very important in India and many festivals and religious holidays begin on a full moon. We decided to make this event an out of body experience. While on the train all of us ate a cookie type cake we baked before we left. We filled each cookie with ganja, the Indian term used for marijuana. When one eats ganja the high lasts longer. In our case, the experienced continued until the next morning.

In Cape Comorin, there is a fort built on the end of the mainland overlooking the ocean at the southernmost tip of the country. We departed from the train just as the effects of the special cake kicked in. A short taxi ride took us to the fort and from there we found our way to our seats. The show was about to begin.

The place where we sat was located on a wall inside the fort. From there we could see the full moon rise out of the ocean in the east and the sunset in the west. On this particular evening, the heavens added a few more props. The clouds seemed to be stacked in strands of four or five horizontal layers on top of each other. This meant the sun needed to pass behind each layer on its' journey into the ocean.

As the sun set, the clouds caught all the colors and reflected the orange, red, and yellow hues of a typical sunset. The difference separating this sun set from others experienced pertained to the sun setting and re-appearing through each layer of cloud. In other words the sun set five times and resurfaced sending all the previously mentioned colors throughout the heavens.

Finally, the sun did its' last descent into the ocean. The clouds held onto their color for another twenty minutes before making their final curtain bow. The second act on this evening of celestial performances still remained.

The moon to the east now started its' ascent into the sky. The cloud layers, contributing to this spectacular sunset, were nonexistent towards the east. The moon captured the orange colors reflected by the sun for the first five minutes of its' journey into the heavens. Soon the all-white moon held the stage doing a solo act. We rested our heads on our sleeping bags and viewed the rest of the show from a horizontal position. To this day the full moonrise and sunset at Cape Comorin remains the most breathtaking heavenly experience I have ever witnessed.

All of a sudden a three or four cannon volley went off in another section of the fort. I jumped to the conclusion that the soldiers who fired the cannons were agreeing with me. They must have thought the performance of sunset and moonrise to be the best one witnessed by mankind. To show their appreciation they decided to acknowledge the event by firing off cannons and drawing attention to this planetary presentation.

I found out the next day the cannons were fired each sunset. Oh well. At least I got to experience the solar, lunar exchange.

We all slept on the hard wall of the fort as the moon crossed the sky and eventually set in the West. The sun rose shortly before the moon set and for about half an hour both solar and lunar bodies remained visible at the same time hovering over separate oceans.

For myself, the Cape Comorin planet event may never be topped. The only way I could see a better solar and lunar show would be from space. Perhaps those private space trips will be running in a few years and if I sell a couple hundred thousand books to pay the round trip fair….. Oops, I forgot. I have vertigo. Never mind.

Chapter 31
Pondicherry

From Cape Comorin, we headed north to another part of India along the eastern coast. Pondicherry, like Goa, used to be a colony of a foreign European country. France controlled the area from 1742 to 1954. Many of the colonies established in the east controlled the accesses to the ocean for trade and shipping. Pondicherry owned such a port and served France well during the colonial period of world history.

Someone in our group heard about the Sri Aurobindo Ashram from other travelers in India. My interest in different spiritual teachers grew the longer I remained on the sub-continent. One cannot escape the impact of the Hindu and Buddhist religions throughout this cultural and spiritual diverse country.

Sri Aurobindo remains as one of those famous spiritual leaders of India's past. He started his Ashram in 1926 with the help of a French woman named Mirra Alfassa. 'The Mother' became her accepted name among her spiritual followers. In April of 1972, she remained the only one of the two founders left. She would leave her body within a year. She died in November of 1973.

Sri Aurobindo became politically involved in the liberation movement to free India from British rule. Like Gandhi he received his education in England. He served as a public servant in India for a number of years but later separated from political life.

He and Mirra started the ashram in Pondicherry to help devotees find their path to God through yoga. Aurobindo wrote many books on spirituality and yoga. His ashram grew to the size of a small village. Many westerners lived in the ashram and practiced the spiritual teachings of Aurobindo and The Mother. (Sri Aurobindo)

When our travel group arrived at the compound we took the guided tour of the grounds. I came across another traveler I previously met while in Nepal months before. I knew her only as another westerner enjoying the city of Kathmandu and talked to her on a few occasions at a restaurant. She joined the community in March and planned a life for herself at the Ashram, using the spiritual practice of Sri Aurobindo. I met many westerners traveling throughout India in the 70s practicing the spiritual insights taught by different gurus following diverse religious practices.

During the tour one of the Ashram devotees approached me. He was an older man who appeared to be in a position of authority at the compound. He wanted to know about my past and previous education. I asked several questions while on the tour and showed a positive interest in the community. At the end of the tour, he offered me the opportunity to become a teacher in the school at the Ashram. I said I would think about it. I still possessed the travel bug and such a commitment at the moment interfered with the wanderlust within.

This event marked the second time I was approached and asked to become a teacher in the East. The Universe seemed to know something I did not. I kept receiving guidance but again I turned away. Not until 1985 did I finally catch up with the truth about myself, and what I would be doing for my life's work.

Later that day 'The Mother' made a daily appearance from her apartment balcony where she lived to bless the followers and visitors gathered to see her. She presented as frail and thin. She dressed in a white Sari waving her arms and hands in a gesture of blessing. The ritual felt calming and soothing.

The woman I met in Nepal, who decided to live at the Ashram, could be still living in Pondicherry today. She also must have an interesting life story to tell if she ever chose to do so.

After leaving Pondicherry, our small group went north to a small town called Mahabalipuram. We found a surf break next to a temple right on the edge of the ocean. Devotees, coming to the temple to pray, lined up on the wall in front of the temple in order to watch Don surf the waves. By the time I took a turn on the surfboard the crowd dispersed and return to their worship rituals. I still could not surf as well as Don using the short board so my rides were quick in length.

Later in the day Don told me he broke up with Katie and did not want to be with her. I became a little concerned about her being alone in the middle of India by herself. I remember seeing her with a young man the next day and I felt relieved. A travel partner meant she would not be alone in India. I did not see Katie again.

In 2011 I found out from Katie what happened to her. She lives in Hawaii and I found her, via Donnie, who gave me a phone number. Her explanation of the breakup told me she decided to break from Don. She felt the treatment she received from him became unhealthy. The man with whom I saw her with the day after the breakup told Katie about Ramana Maharshi's Ashram not far from where we were in India. She decided to go there for a few days to meditate and regroup. She did so and continued her travels in India by herself. Katie also brought her spiritual practice back to the states and continues even today in Hawaii.

Chapter 32
Shiva's Mountain

While in Mahabalipuram, we received information about a town called Tiruvannamalai. A short bus ride took us to the Indian community located in the state of Tamil Nadu. The community maintains a holy temple dedicated to Lord Shiva. A mountain named Arunachala stands near the holy temple. Lord Shiva is said to have gone into the mountain when he stopped living among humans.

A story came to my attention regarding Arunachala through another traveler. The tale is connected with the space program. On one of the space flights, a report said the astronauts spotted an unidentified light source coming from the earth. The origin of the light could not be explained. The space team wrote down the coordinates. The mysterious light came from Mount Arunachala, the mountain where Shiva retired into centuries before. I never researched the narrative to see if there existed any documented truth. I will just let it be what it is, an interesting story.

Another traveler joined Don and me on our short trip to Tiruvannamalai. We stayed at a small Hindu ashram in the middle of the town and ate the evening meal with the priest of the ashram. Our rent included a donation to the keeper of the house and attendance to the morning prayers led by the Brahman holy leader.

Lunch also became a part of the stay. Tortilla like bread called Chapatti, a type of un-leavened flat bread, is used as a scoop to eat the vegetables. When you eat in India use only your right hand. Everyone knows where your left hand has been. For the reader who does not know what I am talking about here is a clue. Toilet paper is generally not used in India or in most Eastern countries. Combine water with the left hand and you start to understand how this toilet duty is performed.

While walking around town on the first day we came across a Sadhu sitting on a wall. He seemed to be waiting for us. He spoke fluent English without the heavy Indian accent. He appeared well educated. If I guessed the history of this particular holy man I would say he came from a wealthy family and decided to live the spiritual life of a Sadhu. This type of separation from the world of means in order to live a spiritual life is not uncommon in India. This is the exact path Buddha chose.

The man wore his hair long but not coiled on the top of the head like other holy men. He appeared to be in his fifties and did not show signs of a difficult life. The complexion of his skin told me he probably came from the northern part of India where skin colors are lighter. The southern Indian colors range from a dark brown to black. Dressed in white, he displayed a non-threatening presence.

The Sadhu began a conversation with us. Within minutes he persuaded us to join him on a tour of the town. The journey included holy sites and a cave where a western Sadhu lived dressed only in a loincloth. He greeted us with his English accent.

In the evening the Sadhu tour guide planned on going up to Mt. Arunachala to meditate and chant during the night. He invited us to go with him. We all agreed not knowing what we were committing ourselves to or what would happen.

The Sadhu met us about an hour before sunset and started up the mountain. Mt. Arunachala was covered by large boulders and reminded me of the rocky hills landscape around Ramona, CA. The climb took about half an hour and the Sadhu found his cave about a third of the way up the mountain. He retreated into the cave with no instructions for his brand new followers. We could hear him began his chanting and meditation rituals from within the mountain retreat.

We all stood there left alone on a mountain where Shiva supposedly went into centuries before. What if Shiva decided to come out and instead of finding followers he found us. Three un-suspecting Americans just sitting there asking ourselves,

"What are we doing here?"

Shiva could get a little pissed.

I decided to try sitting for a while not knowing really how to meditate. I eventually tried to sleep on a large, hard stone. The bed held no comfort. I slept little during the night. The mountain seemed to be pulsating energy and the setting was dialed in so high the earth seemed to visually move. I saw waves of energy, much like heat waves, rising off the rocks. A low humming noise seemed to fill our ears.

Large black Ravens found everywhere in India, became our alarm clock as the sun rose. We gathered ourselves and headed down the mountain, never seeing the Sadhu again. Something appeared to be generating a power source inside Mt. Arunachala. The three of us chose not to be the brave explorers and try to find out what this energy source came from.

For the next three days, I suffered from headaches. Whatever I did to rid myself of the throbbing failed. I tried Indian balms and other remedies but none of the local medicines eased the pain. On day two we decided to make the walk around the mountain to pay respects to Shiva. Worshippers did the journey each day and hundreds of these followers of Shiva filled the road around Mt. Arunachala. I hoped the pilgrimage would distract my attention away from the pain filling my head. Altogether the journey stretched eight miles in length.

While on the Shiva pilgrimage I needed to relieve myself. I did not plan on the journey being so long and I learned from other pilgrims we still were miles from town. Nowhere did I see a relief station. I jogged ahead of my two friends because the situation became difficult. I really needed to go.

Here is a good travel tip. When in India or other eastern countries make an effort to know where the bathrooms are located. Foreign foods have a way of reacting in a tourist's stomach without warning. Knowledge of a WC is powerful. I eventually found one near town, relieved myself and headed down the main road back towards the temples.

Unknown to the three of us a special parade began in the morning near the main temple. Since we left for the walk at sunrise and I returned to town ahead of my friends, I arrived just in time to view the spectacle. What I am about to describe is not something the reader will ever see in their lifetime. It will not be featured in a travel pamphlet for India and no tour bus will take Europeans to this parade.

I noticed people standing on the side of the road waiting for something to come their way. Soon a group of young girls dressed up in costumes worn on holy days came down the road. I continued to walk towards the oncoming parade. The next participants, young men in loincloths, wore body paint covering their legs and upper torso. Red stripes of paint streaked across their foreheads. They were barefoot and their long hair indicated they could be devotees of Shiva.

I possessed no previous knowledge to prepare myself for what followed. Across the chest and arms of the young Sadhus hung small balls on strings. The strings were attached to the body with fishhooks and pierced into and through the skin. White powder covered the entry and exit wounds.
The white substance probably stopped the bleeding. The balls hung in rows along the arms and throughout the upper torso. At least forty of these devotees paraded by.

As I looked back towards the temple from where the parade started I noticed something much larger moving towards me. A massive float with a statue of one of the deities slowly made its' way along the route. In front of the float, a bull of a man pulled the large wagon behind. This powerfully built man, like the other devotees, wore only a loincloth. His short stature along with football player size legs and massive chest and arms made him a perfect candidate for the position he held. The glazed look in his eyes told me he took an opiate of some kind to help kill the pain.

As the float passed me I saw how the man and the float connected. From the wheeled cart stretched four ropes. At the end of the ropes, four massive hooks were attached. Two of the hooks entered and exited the loose skin covering the shoulder blades of this human horse. The other two spikes did the same in the fleshy part of the hip area. White powder again covered the wounds to stop any bleeding.

Each time the devotee stopped and restarted the skin around the hook areas on his body would pull away from the torso. The stopping and starting happened several times while in front of me and I thought the skin might rip right off the bone. No tearing occurred and the float continued down the parade route.

My camera remained in my hand but I never took a picture. I stood on the street watching the end of the parade pass. I was stunned and barely believed the event I just witnessed. I failed to record any of the parade.

I forgot about my headache from my experience on the mountain days before. I observed a part of India only Indians see. Southern India remains the mysterious region of the continent where such rituals and ceremonies continue today.

India is on the cutting edge of becoming one of the most advanced technological countries in the world. The ceremony just witnessed is another part of India only a devotee of Shiva or other deities could understand. The experience reminded me of my first step into the Medina in Morocco. Little has changed for thousands of years in remote areas where the ancient culture of India still exists. The encounter definitely placed me out of my comfort zone of understanding. Seeing and accepting the ceremonial parade remained my only option.

Don and our other friend returned to the ashram an hour after I arrived. They both missed the parade and the man-drawn cart. They also failed to witness the younger devotees with the hanging balls hooked into their skin. I guess the event played out for me alone. Even today the incident forever remains engraved in my memories of strange encounters.

Chapter 33
Paramhansa Yogananda

Don and I left for Puri in the state of Orissa on the Bay of Bengal. Our other friend decided on another direction. Many people in the 60s and 70s have heard about or read, the "Autobiography of a Yogi" by Paramhansa Yogananda. The book tells the life of a young Indian boy who fell in love with the practice of meditation and Yoga. With the help of his teacher, Sri Yukteshwarji, he reached the level of Paramhansa or master.

Paramhansa Yogananda became the first teacher to bring the practice of Kriya Yoga to the West. Yogananda learned from his master in the city of Puri. The followers of Yukteshwarji, the guru of Yogananda, still maintained his ashram in the town. We intended to visit the ashram and learn about meditation. (Paramhansa Yogananda)

Don practiced meditation, using Kriya Yoga techniques, back in the States. He wanted to become ordained as a devotee while in Puri. We found a hotel near the beach and decided to stay for a week.

The ashram, a simple building located in the middle of town, did not take long to find.

Many westerners read the popular book by Yogananda and visited his guru's home. All we needed to do was ask a westerner in town and they seemed to know the location of the building. Our first trip to the ashram took me to the grave of Sri Yukteshwarji located in the rear of the garden. I walked into the garden and sat for a while by the tomb. I found the experience calming and peaceful. I thought to myself,

"Maybe there is something to this meditation thing."

The next four nights we returned to the ashram and meditated with the Yogi master. He gave us no instructions so I practiced a breathing technique a college friend showed me a few years before. The master, a retired teacher, ran the ashram. He trained several young devotees who lived with him. At night a regular attendance of Indian men came to meditate.

During the day Don and I would explore beach spots and surf if the waves looked any good. There were several places we found where we could paddle out and catch waves. The sight of surfing always drew a crowd and by the time we finished many Indian citizens gathered in groups to view and discuss this western sport of surfing. We surfed the waves of the ocean in the day and rode the thoughts of our minds at night.

After four days in Puri, Don asked the master if he could be initiated into the Kriya Yoga practice. The Guru seemed a little shocked at such a request. He seemed serious regarding meditation and he explained to Don the practice of Kriya Yoga and initiation into the practice could not be handed out to anyone just because they asked. The master told Don he would have to sit in meditation for 12 hours in one session before he could be considered. The next day Don wanted to try doing the 12-hour meditation. I think he lasted two hours sitting on his bed in the hotel. Don seemed disappointed and did not bring up the subject again.

The practice of meditation and Yoga is a journey and not something happening in a 12-hour sitting. For myself, the time in Puri became a starting point. I remained open to exploring meditation and see the direction it would take me. The experience in the Ashram became a directional shift in my spiritual quest.

I am grateful for Don wanting to go there and practice Kriya Yoga.

When we decided to leave Puri, Don chose to leave his surfboard at the Ashram. Carrying it on trains reached a point of being an inconvenience. He thought other travelers coming by the ashram could use it. They could share the joy of surfing as we did. He wanted to go into the Himalayan Mountains and bringing a surfboard made no sense.

That surfboard should be bronzed. Don and I must have been the first to surf in India. The dates were 1971-1972. If anyone ever goes by the ashram in Puri please let me know if the surfboard is still there. I surfed again in 1974 when I returned to Puri on my way to Australia but this later adventure unfolds later in the book.

My visa in India approached the exit date and I started to plan my return to Europe. Before heading down to Goa in November I purchased Indian clothing and articles to sell on the beaches of Greece. I stored the items at the train station in Bombay in a locked suitcase. I needed to return to Bombay before heading west.

Don did not go to Nepal when he first came to India. He planned on going there now before returning to the states. We parted paths in Calcutta after staying a few nights in the middle of the city. He continued north and I again climbed aboard the Calcutta to Bombay express. I looked forward to seeing India one more time while riding the train

back to Bombay. If a traveler truly wants to see India one should travel on this cross-country route. The journey goes right through the heart of India.

A scene in the movie 'Ghandi' takes this most famous leader of India on a similar journey. He travels all over India by train to get in touch with the country he never knew. The train traveler today will see India still as an agrarian society. Progress is being made in the world standing of technological advancement but a country still needs to feed its' population. Farmers will always have a job.

India, since my last visit in 1975, increased its' population from 450 million to 1 billion. The traveler must not be in a rush. The large human count makes the most mundane chores like shopping a rigorous challenge. I discovered a thing called patience while visiting cities throughout this country. Shopping, postal duties, banking and touring cannot be completed in a day. Long lines in India demand time to complete each chore. Travelers may feel a little claustrophobic so be prepared.

Second class on the cross-country train ride is my preferred level of travel. I could still order meals served on the train or I could buy food from the many vendors who sold their vegetarian dishes from the train station platforms. I enjoyed the contact with the population and at the same time I traveled in a semi-private room shared with only five other passengers. Each of us was provided with fold down beds at night and a nice hot cup of chai in the morning. Neem tree sticks could be purchased from vendors at different stations and the job of brushing one's teeth Indian style kept the choppers clean and healthy.

A short note regarding a Neem tree stick should be added. This small twig is purchased to clean one's teeth. The end is first chewed so that the small fibers in the branch become soft and mushy. The Neem fibers are then used to polish and remove any food items on the surface of the teeth. Flossing is another practice in dental hygiene and this practice involves the purchase of a string fiber. String or stick? You choose.

Indian Sadhu at a train station in India.

The journey does take two and a half days but the adventure is worth it. Small villages and larger cities are on the route along with the multitude of farmland and crops of mostly rice, the staple food of India. The colors of India are ever present along with the different types of people ranging from wealthy businessmen to wandering Sadhus. India has it all and a good camera can capture the country from a railroad car.

After retrieving my Indian suitcase at the Bombay train station I again purchased a second-class ticket back to New Delhi. Loaded down with Indian clothing and handicrafts, I needed to travel with the middle class in order to protect my purchases. Third class can be very chaotic and is only recommended for short trips. On longer train rides in third class, wandering hands can make their way into luggage not belonging to them.

Upon my arrival in New Delhi, I needed a place to stay for a few days. I grew tired of the over- populated capital of India and the countryside would allow me the peace and quiet needed while recovering from the many miles just completed. A fellow traveler told me to take a certain bus to the small town of Mehrauli. I followed the directions to a Buddhist monastery outside of town. Located within the walls of the complex westerners could sleep in the dorm like rooms for little money. The path through a field leading to the domain contained large numbers of wild peacocks. When I asked the Monk at the monastery why there were so many of these birds living just outside the walls, he said,

"The peacocks kill and eat the many cobras inhabiting the tall grassy field."

"Oh great," I thought. "I have to go through the field every time I go into town to shop."

The peacocks seemed to do a good job eating the cobra population because the only snakes seen by me while in India were in a Snake Charmers basket. These charmer snakes usually were fangless and presented no danger to the tourist watching the five-minute dance to the flute pipe music.

My stay at the Buddhist compound lasted a week. The cheap rent attracted many kinds of western travelers. Six French drug addicts happened to be using one of the dorm rooms for their shoot-ups and getting high on their morphine vacation stay. Morphine could be purchased over the counter without any prescription in India in 1972. Every night the druggies tied off their arms exposing any veins still usable in order to get the painkillers into their blood and rush to their brains. I kept a low profile with these short timers of life. My guess is they would not see the 80s at the drug pace they lived. I felt only disgust for such being wasting this precious thing called life.

The atmosphere in the dorm rooms felt inundated by the heavy negative energy provided by the behavior of the morph heads. Late in the evening on the fourth day, the door opened to the kitchen room shared by the monastery inhabitants. In walked a western Sadhu accompanied by another man who appeared to be a disciple follower. The thick cloud of despair surrounding the morphine high druggies parted and all the talking in the room stopped.

There is a scene in the movie, 'Lord of the Rings', after Gandalf's return as the White Wizard. In the movie, the Hobbits and Gandalf are surrounded by Orcs, which represent evil or the dark side. The White Wizard takes his staff and pounds the base into the ground and a white illumination energy force radiates from the head of the staff sending the dark evil creatures away from the light and its' power.

This exact scene took place in the kitchen of the Buddhist monastery as the Sadhu and his companion entered the room. An energy field surrounded the holy wanderer. It felt similar to the force I experienced with the Sadhus and the Tibetan Nun in Nepal. The junkies parted like the Red Sea in front of Moses and his staff. They retreated to the back of the room where they could observe the two new arrivals from a safe distance. None of the junkies came near the two men and all of them seemed to have lost the power of speech.

As the evening continued more information about this western Sadhu emerged. He was originally from Germany and lived in India for the past twelve years. For ten years, after taking the path of a wandering holy man, he practiced meditation and other rituals common among this sect of worshipers. His uncut hair remained twisted and piled upon his head and the twelve-year long beard reaching to the middle of his stomach showed a slight graying. I guessed his age to be around forty. His spiritual path must have begun in his late twenties.

A few of the monastery inhabitants asked questions regarding spiritual matters. I am not sure if the inquiries were meant to find a weakness in his practice or they were coming from a place of real knowledge seeking. His answers cut right through the doubt lingering in the room. He spoke with authority and answered any questions the audience presented. The junkies could not find a hole in the armor of the Sadhu and eventually they retreated to their dorm room for the duration of the evening along with their negative energy.

The Sadhu and companion prepared and ate their meal in silence. A few hours later both of them retired to bed. The men must have risen early in the morning because they were gone when I awoke. I have met westerners who have committed to the Buddhist practice and became a monk or nun but this was the first westerner I met who chose the path of a wandering Sadhu.

I left a day later and started my journey back to the west. I completed my stay in India for as long as my visa would allow. After six months in India, I needed to return to the west. I seemed to be operating on overload and I could not fit another adventure into my brain. My interest in meditation and meeting different people who made the practice their life held a strong desire to find out more. I knew I needed to return to India and find a practice I could use in my life.

Chapter 34
Return to the West

In the spring of 1972 the India – Pakistan border remained closed. The war ended months before but each side stood determined to shut out the other in the game called "who will blink first." Many western travelers were trapped in India and could not use the overland route to Europe. I traveled from New Delhi to the border and waited in Amritsar. The Sikh community at the Golden Temple served lunch to many westerners in the same situation I found myself in. Waiting.

The two governments of India and Pakistan saw the buildup of western travelers along the border becoming a problem. For ten days both sides of the crossing opened and many westerners, including myself, passed into Pakistan. From Pakistan, we all took a train to the Afghan border and escaped the conflicted area. A bus ride up the Khyber Pass returned us to the capital of Afghanistan.

Kabul remained in its' rugged, unchanged condition. I was in no hurry to leave Afghanistan this time. The country took no part in the Indian-Pakistan war and remained undamaged. Conflict would not break out until Christmas Eve of 1979 when Soviet troops invaded the country. That war lasted until February 15, 1989 when the Russians finally pulled out. Afghanistan took down a world power in 1989 and many say it bankrupted Russia. I wonder if Afghanistan is about to financially bring down another powerful world nation today?

In Kabul, I returned to the same hotel, Sigis, with the large chess pieces and the continuous battle played out in the front yard. Many young travelers from the West never leave Afghanistan. Drugs are cheap and plentiful and the cost of living is only a few dollars a day. I traveled to see the world and not to become a statistic. Such drugged out travelers either died in the east or entered rehab if they were lucky enough to live.

I tried to get a bus to Bamyan in the middle of Afghanistan. Bamyan is the place where Buddhist monks carved huge statues of Buddha out of a mountainside. April held no snow on the ground in the Afgan valleys but the mountain passes still were blocked. In Afghanistan, no snowplows can be found in order to clear the mountain passes. The Afghanistan government waits for Mother Nature to melt away winter. This year the snowfall appeared to be heavy. Bus drivers to Bamyan said it might not be until May before vehicles could get through.

The two biggest Buddha statues of Bamyan are said to have been 180 feet and 121 feet high. They date back to the sixth century when Buddhist monks carved them. At one time Buddhism remained the religious practice throughout India, Pakistan, Afghanistan and down through South East Asia.

Before the Taliban destroyed the statues in 2001, the Mullah Mohammed Omar made a decree. The huge monuments were to be left alone because they brought in a good income from tourists and traveling Buddhists. By March of 2001 the Taliban, a non-inclusive sect of the Muslim religion took power. All statues and idols needed to be destroyed. The Buddhas of Bamyan would not escape the religious wrath of the Taliban. Their destruction stopped the flow of tourists and travelers to the region. Buddhism lost one of their great treasures in the world.

Another possible place to visit in Afghanistan was the town of Mazari Sharif. The town lay to the northwest of Kabul. I and another adventurous friend decided to take the bus ride to this city and explore the area. The ride to Mazari Sharif took several hours. We crossed no mountain passes and the roads remained clear.

Mazari Sharif is a much smaller town than the capital of Kabul. Farming and the production of hash and opium remained the source of income in the region. Fields surrounded the town but the cool spring weather kept any planting in limbo.

I and another traveler stayed for three or four days walking around the ruins of the old city leveled by Genghis Khan. Before the destruction of the old city, the historical beginning unfolded in the 12th century. Ali bin Abi Talib, a cousin and son in law of the prophet Muhammad, was secretly buried where the old city stood. To honor him a mosque and city grew around the site. The closest city of Balkh became a neighbor community to Mazari Sharif.

All that remained of the city were the tall mud walls slowly eroding away. While walking around this ancient ruin I looked from a section of the clay barrier down into the non-existent remains of the city. A camel caravan with ten or fifteen beasts of burden used the city barriers as a windbreak while camping overnight. Nothing remained indicating life ever existed in the enclosed compound.

On one of my photo outings, I discovered how dangerous being a foreigner could be in Afghanistan. The event unfolded while returning to the hotel after a walk outside the village. When a traveler finds him or herself in a situation with the potential to become ugly, remember to maintain a cool head and take the path of least resistance.

I happened to be turning a corner on a rutted road on the outskirt of a residential part of the city. Approaching me were two women surrounded by their children after a day of shopping. The Burqa or outer garment, worn by the Afghan women, was pulled back over their heads revealing their faces. The tent-like garb covers the entire body of a woman in Afghanistan and is never removed until she returns to her home.

The women must have been near their homes and were not expecting a foreigner to be coming around the corner. They quickly pulled the Burqas back over their faces and were again hidden from the foreigner approaching them. Only a small net in the Burqa around the eye sockets remained as an opening. The small area enabled the women to see and breath while walking.

The mothers seemed angry with me for having observed their exposed head and face. I could tell by the tone in their voice when they passed the event was a major taboo. I kept walking.

Twenty feet separated me from the group of shoppers when rocks began hitting the ground near my body. The young boys accompanying their mothers prepared to defend the family honor by stoning the infidel. These boys were not much older than eight or nine. Lucky for me their aim sucked. I turned around to face them and thought about making a charge. This tactic worked with the young Sherpa children in Namche Bazaar.

It is times like this one must realize,

"I am in a foreign country and I better be sure I make good decisions."

Instead of rushing at the children like a crazed Oakland Raider fan hoping to scare the crap out of them, I kept walking away. I increased my pace. I needed to lengthen my distance from the young boys. Eight-year-olds attempting to make their first honor killing could become quite nasty.

The children did not follow nor did an incensed adult male come running around the corner trying to complete the stoning attempt made by the young rock throwers. I still needed fifteen minutes before reaching the safety of the hotel. Once inside the hotel wall, I relaxed. I left the next day on the bus back to Kabul, feeling lucky to tell the tale.

I did not stay long in Kabul when I returned from Mazari Sharif. I finished my tour of Afghanistan and now the beaches of Greece called to me. I looked forward to selling my goods to the tourists from the States and Europe. I made one more stop in Kandahar to shop for some Afghan shirts seen on my way through to India the first time. After an afternoon of haggling, I completed the transactions and set out for Herat the next morning.

Afghan elders discussing a tribal matter.

By the time I reached Herat a bug caught up with me and I became sick for about three or four days. The illness limited me to staying in bed and eating a diet of fruit and naan (bread) while drinking chi (tea). As I lay there I watched a swallow family feed their newly born babies in the nest built on the inside of the door entrance to the room. Afghan hotels, in Herat in 1972 blended a little nature with the accommodations provided. I would not award even a half star to the hotels in this dirt-poor border town.

The trip through Iran passed uneventfully. I held little interest in Persia at the time but I now wish I traveled to a few cities off the beaten track to experience more of the culture. I believe the tension felt by travelers passing through Iran did not make for a long visit. The worry I am talking about seemed to be amongst the middle class regarding the Shaw of Iran. I will dwell on this subject at a later time.

From the border of Iran and Turkey, I caught a train to the capital of Ankara located several hundred miles to the east of Istanbul. There must be some reason countries like Turkey and Brazil put their capitals away from population and economic centers. I could also say the same for the U.S. who chose Washington D.C. over New York City. When a country plans a new capital there must be plenty of room for the war memorials and other centers of culture reminding the citizens what their armies died for.

Turkey after WWI became an independent Republic under the first president, Mustafa Kemal Ataturk. He made many reforms in Turkey including the western clothing styles worn by men and women. The country's lean toward the West began under the leadership of Ataturk. Today the country is trying to become a part of the European Common Market. (Turkey)

Istanbul also made some wonderful changes to its' present day appearance. The government spent money on roads, public transportation and cleaned up the main city and tourist areas. The Blue Mosque remains the most wonderful sight in Istanbul and it should be a part of any Eastern Europe tour package.

Chapter 35
Greece, The Summer of 1972

I did not remain more than two days in Istanbul. The month of May arrived and the warmer weather brought back the memories of the Greek beaches and wonderful food. Instead of going directly to Mykonos I decided to try selling my goods on another island.

A map from a friend in India directed me to a cave on the island of Paros. The same friend accompanied our small travel group when we witnessed the sunset at Cape Comorin in Southern India. The cave was located just out of town and provided enough room for a small flock of sheep. Caves throughout the Greek islands protected the Shepherds and their sheep during the rainy season.

I lasted about three evenings in the cave. A pack- rat living there kept running across my chest during the night. He seemed to be telling me this cave was his and he wanted it to himself. I agreed and checked into a small hotel full of westerners from the States. The Americans were followers of some famous singer whose name I cannot remember. They were waiting for his return to Paros. I think the term used for such young adults is "groupies."

Two years of traveling and seeing the world began to quiet me on the inside. I reflected a lot about the things I viewed and experienced. Having just returned from India, I presented as a recluse. I separated myself from the mundane conversations going on between other American travelers coming to Europe for the first time. The first month back in the West became a period of adjustment. Self-evaluation and reflection are not uncommon after nine months of travel in the East.

Not many European tourists came to Paros. I carried a lot of Eastern clothing and jewelry to be sold. Mykonos remained a destination for young travelers in the early 70s so I returned to the island to live and sell my wears. I took the boat ride to the main beach called Paradise Beach where I first met the two brothers who told me about India and trekking in Nepal. When I finally reached Paradise Beach the brothers could not be found. Some other Jewish friends of theirs already staked out a spot on the restaurant beach selling the same items I carried. They just returned from India as well and were selling the desired eastern treasures to the newly arrived American youth.

Most of the young people on Mykonos in the month of May appeared to be New York Jewish men and women either on their way to Israel to work on a Kibbutz or just returning from these farms. In 1972 the Kibbutz life remained important if you were young and Jewish. Life on a Kibbutz sounded like a great experience. The people on the farms worked hard and played hard. The stories being told by those just returning from Israel almost convinced me I should become a Jew so I too could have such an experience.

I moved to the Gay beach two days later. This beach lay just over the next hill in the next sandy cove. I preferred to take the boat instead of trying to lug all my wears overland. The other merchants from India selling their items did not want competition on Paradise Beach. I felt there were plenty of tourists on this island to go around. The Gay community and their beach became a good move for me. The men spent money for Indian shirts, pants and prayer beads. They loved the items from India. Most of the clothes I brought were sold in the first month. A few dresses found their way into a store in the town and were sold on consignment.

My summer in Greece proved to be an adjustment. Being around young westerners from the states held little interest for me. Most of them were in Greece for the first time having left America a few months before. Their idea of summer fun remained the same as the youth living on Ios in 1971. Party, hangover, recover and party again. This lifestyle did not appeal to me then or in Mykonos now.

I eventually connected with a few travelers who just returned from India as well. They did not want to return to the party lifestyle either. One young man named Scotty spent a lot of time in an Ashram and meditation became his practice every morning. We became friends and spent time talking about India and all the wonders this diverse sub-continent offered to the traveler.

Traveling in India changes a person. Both Scotty and I became more reflective in our outlook on life. Many of the westerners returning from India practiced some form of meditation and no longer wanted to indulge in the party lifestyle. My purpose in life and what I could do to make a difference held more importance.

My stay on the Gay beach included working in the restaurant. The eatery was owned by a Greek family and provided the only food in the area. At lunchtime, servers were needed to help feed the hungry beach community. Helping to serve the visiting hordes at lunch meant a free meal at night. Few tourists stayed on the beaches after sunset. They returned to the continuing party in town. For those of us who slept on the beach, our evenings remained quiet and calming.

A dress code did exist at all the Greek beach restaurants. Nudity was fine on the beaches but not where food was served. The Greek Orthodox Church tried to enforce a clothing code but with little success. The local police patrolled the island beaches and sent out a warning boat ahead of them for everyone to get dressed. Ten minutes later when the police arrived everyone was covered and no tickets for nudity needed to be written. Only one woman I noticed who was taking a nap did not get the warning and had to pay a fine.

The Greeks on Mykonos realized a fully enforced dress code would kill tourism. Lots of money came into the pockets of the restaurant owners and fishermen who transported the tourists to these beaches. The way the island Greeks looked at the situation seemed practical. If tourists wanted to take off their clothes while on the beach then so be it. Just keep the nudity on the beach and away from public places.

Chapter 36
Side Trip to Italy

Toward the end of summer, I decided to travel up through Yugoslavia to Venice and visit my aunt, uncle, and sister. My uncle was a professor at Wake Forest University and taught history to students from the college. The family and students lived in a building owned by the University on the Grand Canal. The students studied Italian and history as well as receiving a cultural experience in Italy.

I left for Venice with a couple of friends wanting to visit a buddy of theirs in Milan. In 1972 hitchhiking remained as a safe means of travel. The journey through Yugoslavia was a trip through several cultures. Muslims and Christians lived together in most of the regions. Years later war would tear this country apart and the different ethnic groups would end up killing each other in the name of religion.

The trip through Yugoslavia took three days. A blond airline stewardess traveling with us helped in getting the attention of drivers. Our group split up before reaching the Italian border. Peter and Yvonne went one way towards Milan and the stewardess accompanied me to Venice. We decided we would all meet up later in Milan.

I arrived in Venice and found the address where Aunt Bonnie, Uncle Cyclone and my sister Louise stayed. Sporting a long beard and matching hair accompanied by a blond airline stewardess must have presented an unusual sight. The hippie traveler in the family finally arrived at the college professor's doorstep.

My aunt did not seem to mind my appearance but I am sure she knew how her husband would react. She sent me downstairs to greet him. She was going for the full shock effect. She was right. Uncle Cyclone almost jumped out of his skin when he saw me. The first comment coming from him,

"How long are you staying?"

I last visited the Covey family in 1964 on my return from Europe after living in Salzburg. Bonnie is the youngest of the sisters on my mother's side of the family. She is the funniest and I believe the smartest of all my aunts. Both of us share a lot of the same political views for the United States.

After a day or two, my uncle calmed down realizing I would not pull a Charles Manson on him and his family. A week later, while preparing to leave for Milan, Uncle Cy tried to talk me into going to Turkey with him at a later date and look for the remains of some early civilization. I tried to explain to him how rugged and tough the people of Eastern Turkey were and he may do much better with a Turkish guide who spoke the language and knew the customs. My plan included a return to India so I declined to lead an expedition into the wilds of Turkey with my college professor uncle.

Before going to Milan to join my other friends from Greece I took a small group of college students from my uncle's Wake Forest student body to the Munich Oktoberfest in Germany. My aunt trusted me to take her daughter and young son, Jonathan, on the journey. We all drank a few beers and stayed overnight in an apartment of some German students we met at the Festival. The next day we took the train back to Venice.

Thinking back on the adventure I am proud of the fact I returned everyone to Venice in one piece.

I left for Milan soon after returning from Germany. I started to think about India again. Summer heat in Greece lessened each day and cool winds started to blow south from northern Europe.

The stay in Milan did not last long. My two friends, Yvonne and Peter, were visiting their gay American friend, Moose. Because of his good looks, Moose became a male model in Europe. For a week I got to experience the life of a cover boy and cover girl in Italy. Beautiful Scandinavian women and good looking men from all over the world made up the group of models vying for photo shoots and magazine covers flooding the European market.

Most of the male models in Milan were gay. The pay for a shoot remained high and the lifestyle was a continuous fiesta. All meals were eaten in the best restaurants of Milan and parties happened nightly. Cocaine kept many of the models awake for days at a time and other drugs helped them sleep when the time came to crash. The modeling world did not interest me and I soon left for Greece to prepare for my return trip back to India.

Chapter 37
Back to India, 1972

During the summer of 1972, I received a letter from an uncle regarding my wealthy grandfather. He willed to all his grandchildren $5000. In the early 70s, this amount equaled a lot of travel money. I invited Yvonne and Peter to come to India with me and I would pay their way. After the Italy trip, we regrouped in Greece, said goodbye to our summer friends and headed to Istanbul to begin the great overland journey.

Neither Yvonne nor Peter had been to Istanbul or any country to the East. I felt like a tourist guide as I directed them to the Blue Mosque, the puzzle ring factory and all the other sights discovered on previous visits. We met a few other travelers heading east while staying at the Pudding Shop hotel in Istanbul. The growing group gathered together on the Asia side of Turkey where we boarded the train to Iran.

Yvonne received her education in a private school in Europe. Her wealthy Swedish mother made sure she received a good start in life. The private girl's school educated young women from all over the world. One of her school friends came from Iran. The Iranian girl's father served as an ambassador to one of the European nations so the family lived in Europe and knew the traditions of the west. Yvonne said her friend lived in Tehran at the present time and she would like to call and visit her.

When we reached Tehran we checked into the same hotel where I previously stayed the year before. The hotel was located in the old part of the city and remained a clean place for western travelers. The men in the old city wore traditional clothing of Iran and women covered their heads with a headscarf. The dress code for the women remained enforced by the vigilant men upholding the religious clothing styles of Iran. The protectors of woman's attire were everywhere and any young girls who let the headscarf slip off their heads in order to show their feminine locks were quickly given a tongue lashing.

Yvonne made a phone call to her friend. We were told she would meet us at our hotel the next morning. I did not have any idea how the Iranian friend would look. Her friend arrived at the hotel around nine o'clock dressed in a western skirt and blouse. She wore no headscarf and she looked like she just stepped off a street in a European city. She greeted Yvonne and introduced herself to us. She spoke perfect English and welcomed us to her country.

The hotel owner watched the exchange between us and made a comment in Persian or Parsi. The comment was directed at our host and created a response I was not prepared for. She spoke to the innkeeper in an angry tone letting us know as well as anyone in a fifty-foot radius she did not agree with the comment made to her.

We were told later the hotel owner called her a western whore because she refused to wear the traditional dress and headscarf worn by every woman in the old part of Tehran. She also did what no traditional woman in Iran would ever do. She defended herself in public against a man and told the owner to,

"Stick it where the sun don't shine."

We left with Yvonne's school friend and went to the modern part of Tehran where the wealthy families lived and shopped. Stores sold European clothes for men and women. The food restaurants and shops sold items one would find in Europe. There were two cultures in Tehran in 1972. They included followers of the Shah and his government employees and the poorer middle class holding onto traditions of strict Muslim dress codes and behavior.

We were invited to visit the home of Yvonne's classmate. The Shah built his palace on a hill overlooking the city. People employed by the government or wealthy citizens siding with the Shah's attempts to move Iran towards a western society lived in homes built on the hill below the palace. Narrow winding streets through the exclusive neighborhood remained guarded and protected from anyone not belonging to the wealthy gated community.

The homes were western in style but nowhere close to the size of wealthy European dwellings. They seemed to have all the modern conveniences of running water, central air and heat but the spacious living did not exist. The mother of the family greeted us and remained gracious during the entire visit. As she relaxed around us real concern about the future of Iran became apparent. She predicted her family and other families following the Shah would be forced to move to the West. She heard via her husband the majority of the population in Iran remained unhappy with the direction the Shah guided Iran. The people wanted to return to a more traditional Muslim culture.

Within six years the prediction of the mother came true. The revolution happened and strict leaders enforcing Muslim law returned to power. I do not know how many of the followers of the Shah escaped before the change but I believe those who could leave did.

Many left behind died in the name of religion and social change.

In 2009 a second revolution began in Iran. I believe from watching the news the tables have turned for the fundamentalists who took power in 1978. The religious conservative leaders barely held onto the power led by the population. By using force against its' citizens and imprisoning the opposition the religious right looks to be in the same situation as the Shah in 1978. This battle is not over and will be played out in the years to come.

After a few more days in Iran, we finally got our visas for Afghanistan. We said goodbye to our Iranian hosts. They were gracious and welcoming and I wish them all the best. We headed to Mashhad and the beautiful Mosque I described on the first overland journey. Yvonne gained entrance to the Mosque by putting a shawl over her head while Peter and I waited outside and observed the Blue Mosque of Mashhad from the outside.

Heart was the first Afghan town across the border and it shocked Peter and Yvonne to the same degree it did to me on my first visit. There is something haunting about poor third world countries seen for the first time. Mud walls and poor living conditions put a different perspective onto a traveler's ideas of the world and where they came from. I no longer view my lifestyles in the west in the same light before coming to Afghanistan. After arriving at a poor country most travelers can see how the west seems like the pot gold at the end of the rainbow.

We all did the usual camel rides and walks around the town. After a couple of days, we prepared for the bus ride across this desert country and on to Kabul. I knew the capital of Afghanistan would be more interesting than Herat and the hotels a lot cleaner.

I recently saw a news video of Herat dated 2009. The city resembled nothing of the Herat of 1972. The news story mentioned Iran pouring much- needed aide into the town and building up its' economy. The streets were paved. Cars and buses fill the avenues as the main transportation and no evidence of camels and donkeys could be found. I am glad for the needed changes Iran made in Afghanistan and at the same time I am thankful I experienced Herat before the changes.

Chapter 38
Taliban, the Beginning. Maybe

On the morning we boarded the bus to Kandahar and Kabul I broke the one rule I lived by when eating food in Afghanistan. I bought a meat dish from a roadside cook. Because of time restrictions I could not find any bread or fruit, the only foods I felt safe to eat. Yvonne and Peter must have eaten something else in town because they did not want any of the meal. When eating any meat dishes in Afghanistan in 1972 there are no food warnings posted saying,

"This meal could be hazardous to your health."

We entered the bus and took our seats. The bus held only twenty-five passengers. The seats allowed two people together with a row down the middle of the bus for entering and exiting. Yvonne and Peter sat together behind me. I sat with an Afghan man wearing a black turban.

The trip is about six hours to Kandahar with a lunch stop half way. The Afghan countryside is bare with only sandy soil and plenty of rocks. Few trees grew in the desert land. The lack of vegetation usually means the forests have been cut down for firewood. Replanting is not a high priority in a Third World country.

About 45 minutes into the trip something began to happen in my stomach. This situation may have been the beginning of a possible change as to how Afghans feel about Westerners. A bubbling sound started deep in my bowls like a science lab experiment where two substances, when mixed together, cause a chemical reaction. The noises continued and with each bubble, gas was released in my stomach. I sat in my seat and could see my belly starting to expand.

The reaction continued for the next hour. My midsection persisted in its' outward growth. Here I sat on a bus full of Afghans. I did not speak the language and I remained at a complete loss as to the remedy for my plight. Even if I did ask the driver to pull over so I could relieve myself no bushes or rocks existed for privacy. I would become the only roadside show for everyone on the bus. The situation escalated.

I knew I needed a divine intervention because I could not conjure up any ideas on my own. I required something beyond my human mind. No one but me knew my situation so far. I kept the window open to allow any gas smell to escape. The pain continued and I continued praying for a miracle.

All of a sudden a voice like thought came to me. I knew at once the message arrived from a higher power because there was no way I could come up with such a remedy on my own. The internal voice asked,

"What is the worst thing that can happen?"

I knew right away the question became my answer. The worst should happen and I needed to prepare for the outcome.

I prepared for the outcome. First I tightened my belt on the Levi jeans I wore to seal off any possible escape route. I grabbed my pants and tightened the material just above the kneecaps. I squeezed to seal off any possible seepage. I completed all the necessary steps before proceeding. I didn't need to think about the next step any longer.

I released everything in my oversized midsection. The ill-fated breakfast happened hours ago. The buildup since the breakfast exceeded any Thanksgiving dinner on memory. If this instant compared to the moment of giving birth then I know what a two-hour pregnancy felt like.

The pant legs filled first. Liquid always flows from a higher elevation to a lower one. Luck played a part in the disaster. Instead of wearing my older jeans with the many patches, I put on my newer pair of denims that morning. Can you imagine the seepage through the patched pants?

The seal at the knees held. No longer hurting I sat back in my chair as sweat poured off my forehead. The relief I felt outweighed any possible discomfort or grossness. I sat in total surrender to the moment. As we rode through the Afghanistan countryside I started to enjoy the trip and was no longer in misery.

Ten minutes passed. The chemical experiment in my stomach started up again. The extreme pain I experienced minutes before did not scare me.

"Bring it on," I said to myself.

I already traveled to the mountaintop and I returned. I sat in my seat soaked in the worst possible outcome. I laughed at any repeat experience. My stomach refilled but not to the previous level of discomfort. I still maintained more room in my pants and I did not hesitate to fill the space.

By now the Afghani man next to me knew something was not right. He seemed to be edging towards the end of his seat. His nose gave him hints he needed to move. He now sat with his feet in the aisle facing the opposite side of the bus. I could only imagine what thoughts filled his head.

After twenty minutes more of travel the bus started to slow down. We were arriving at a small town along the route where lunch could be purchased. Yvonne and Peter remained clueless as to my mishap. When I asked,

"Peter, can I borrow a pair of your pants?" they started to piece the scenario together.

Peter handed me a pair of cord pants from his backpack. I lifted my right elbow so he could place them under my armpit. I could not retrieve my own extra pants because my hands were in a death grip holding back the flood. Any lessening of the tension above my kneecaps meant sure disaster.

When the bus stopped my Afghan seat partner ran to the front of the bus and made his exit before any other one on the bus. Hunger could not make someone leave a bus so quickly. His desire to create a separation between his nose and my body must have been the driving force moving his feet so quickly.

The lunch stop town was located next to a river and the bus stopped about 200 yards from its' bank. I departed last from the bus with Peter's pants under one armpit and still holding my pants at the kneecaps. By now Yvonne and Peter knew my plight. Holding back laughter they asked for more details. I chose not to explain the story in depth and made my way to the front of the bus.

I told my two travel partners I could not eat right now and I would meet them back at the bus after lunch. I headed to the river still bent over and keeping the damn secure with the power grip on my knees.

Women were walking up from the river with their fresh load of clean laundry and found me quite amusing.

'What could this westerner be doing?' seemed to be written in their expressions.

I walked by gripping my trousers and bent over with another pair of pants under my armpit. By now I held no room for the emotion of embarrassment. All I could focus was a trip to the river and washing the disaster of breakfast away.

The clean up unfolded quite easily. I found a grassy slope leading down to the river. The flat grassy spot looked like the location where the women who just passed me washed their clothes. I dropped the clean pants on the bank and entered the water wearing everything I wore at that moment. Nothing would escape the washing I planned. I even brought a bar of soap and within ten minutes I cleaned and rinsed everything connected with the ordeal.

No women were washing clothes so I managed to change quickly and return to the bus before the departure time.

I returned to the bus and found my seat just as my travel partners returned from lunch. The bus departed and as we traveled through the warm desert countryside I was able to dry my jeans by holding them out the window of the bus. Within fifteen minutes they were completely free from any moisture and ready for me to put back on at the next stop in Kandahar.

Thinking back about the mishap I felt the incident might have caused the black-turbaned Afghan passenger much more stress than anyone else on the journey. When the bus pulled away my seat partner did not return. I assume he lived in this southern Afghan town. In ten years Taliban forces in southern Afghanistan would be organizing against the Russians. In 2002 these same forces would be fighting against American and British troops.

From the view of the Afghan seat partner, the western infidel sitting next to him with gastric sounds coming from the depths of his bowels represented the lowest of non-believers. Such a display of smell and filth should be cleansed from the face of the earth.

The experience by the Black-turbaned Afghan may have been repeated over and over again to his friends and family. His total disgust could be expressed in one simple sentence.

Stinky foreign infidels who ride the bus must be cleansed from the face of the earth.

This statement might have become a rallying cry for the Taliban years later. Perhaps the radical group wears black turbans today in honor of my fellow passenger who survived the ordeal. My seat companion may have become a leader in the ranks of the Taliban repeating his story to followers.

The Afghan also might have become a poster model for Taliban recruitment. Instead of an Uncle Sam poster pointing to the viewer saying, "I Want You", the Afghan poster would show my bus mate with one hand holding his nose while the other hand pointing to the viewer of the poster saying,

"Death to smelly foreigners"

I am not saying any of the events with the Afghan bus passenger happened after he left the bus. I also do not claim the incident on the bus contributed to the factors bringing about such a radical arm of the religion of Islam into existence. That would be too much of a stretch, even for the writer's imagination. Or would it?

Chapter 39
Kabul and India 1972-1973

The rest of the bus ride to Kandahar was uneventful. I dried my own pants by hanging them out the window and letting the warm desert air of Afghanistan do the rest. We stayed overnight in Kandahar and traveled on to Kabul the next day bringing the group to the famous Sigis hotel with the chess board and world class games taking place in the front yard.

I found out the name of Sigis hotel while editing the first edition of this book. Several other travelers who stayed there described the boarding house in their writings just as I did. Many hotels catering to westerners never survived under the Taliban rule. I do not think a chess-playing hotel would have passed the scrutiny of the radical Islamic sect.

Peter and Yvonne enjoyed the journey through Afghanistan as much as I did the first time I traveled through. Third World countries escaping war and invasion from other countries existed in a time period unto themselves. Afghanistan with its' King and warlords ran their communities in harmony. The country functioned closer to a medieval nation in the thirteenth century than anything else.

Even today I question why Russia invaded this piece of real estate with no resources or value. If Afghanistan were left alone it might have become a sought after destination for tourists seeking the unusual. The women in Afghanistan might have transitioned into obtaining more rights as western influences integrated the society.

All the changes in Afghanistan could have come about without war.

The Internet with all its' connections between world nations became a huge building block for shifts in the world. China, India, and Iran are just a few such countries having undergone rapid ideological movement. The people in these regions are demanding more freedoms and choices. The governments holding onto power in these areas cannot keep up with the population's demands. The clashes between the two aspects of a country, the people and the Government, will continue. How the outcome plays out is anyone's guess.

Travel through Pakistan did not take long. The population remained upset over losing the war with India and their eastern holdings. Bangladesh existed as an independent country but Pakistan still held a grudge.

A westerner cannot tell the difference between an Indian and a Pakistani. They are simply the same people. Religions in the two countries created a wall separating the two populations. Hindus do live in Pakistan and Muslims exist in India. How long the two countries allow multiple religions to continue in their countries may be decided in the next few years. The situation is rapidly coming to a head.

Amritsar was our first stop in India and is always a good place to regroup after traveling through Pakistan. I loved going to the Golden Temple. I also found the Sikh religion a wonderful one based on helping and feeding the poor and spreading a helping hand out to others less fortunate. Our stay included our attendance at a wedding, visiting the Temple and preparing for India.

The train ride to New Delhi gives the traveler a picture of the Indian experience. Depending on how adventuresome you felt determined which class of ticket you bought. First class was isolated and comfortable. Soft padded seats and food brought to you by the staff separated the traveler from touching India right outside the window. Second class was also very comfortable and contained soft benches. Food could be purchased from your window at the many stops made along the way. The conditions were usually more crowded than first class.

Third class and the train rooftops held the vast population of India. The bench seats usually made of wooden slats meant the traveler needed to bring cushions to sit on. Most passengers in third class brought their own food so the smell of Indian dishes filled the car. People stood or sat in the hallways and the overflow poured onto the rooftop of the cars. I believe the top of the coaches equaled a free ride because the conductors never went up there to punch tickets.

On my previous trip to India's capital, I mentioned a Buddhist monastery outside of New Delhi. This is where the French junkies and German Sadhu came together for an interesting meeting of the white light and the dark side. I took our group now numbering seven back to the walled compound in order to rest and see another part of Indian history.

The town of Mehrauli contains the Mehrauli Archaeological Park. The park contains the Tomb of Adham Khan and the Qutb Minar built by Sultan Qutbuddin Aibak in 1196. The remains of these structures attracts tourists who take the bus ride out of Delhi daily to the park. The Mogul's architecture can be found throughout India. The Muslims remaining after India and Pakistan split care for these monuments. They live with Sikh and Hindu citizens and do so in peace and harmony. (Qutb Minar)

Gandhi was right. India should have never been separated into different countries based on religion. India maintains a good relationship with all religions. Politics and the English pulling out of India changed the way the two worlds co-existed with each other. The situation of the two countries today is two nuclear powers living next to each other in disharmony.

By the time we reached the monastery all the beds were taken. We received directions to a mausoleum outside the walls of the monastery. We were going to sleep in a graveyard. Our group of Peter, Yvonne, four other travelers and myself still held at seven. We seemed to get along and most of the time there is strength in numbers. We set up sleeping quarters in one of the old tomb rooms and decided to walk back into town for a meal and a drink. Travel can take it out of you and a full stomach usually eases the aches and pains of being on the road.

We returned a few hours later and discovered the most dreaded event a traveler can experience. The skimpy lock on the door to our belongings lay on the ground and our valuables were removed. All our backpacks lay scattered on the ground and clothing covered the floor like a tapestry of many colors. Anything of value no longer remained in the room.

I lost my camera, passport and traveler checks. What was I thinking? When traveling never leave identity documents and money behind no matter where you are. In India and other poor countries, the rule applies ten fold. These are the items keeping you in a country and allowing you to eat while touring. Sleep did not come easily during night.

The next day many of the items holding little value to the robbers were found dumped into the bushes. Passports are not usable to anyone else but the camera and traveler checks were gone. I grieved my loss of the camera. It still contained a whole roll of undeveloped pictures taken in Greece as well as the overland trip through Iran, Afghanistan, and Pakistan. I could get the traveler checks back but not the pictures.

We regrouped and moved into the Buddhist monastery. Safety lay behind the compound walls. The process of getting traveler checks back in India took a long period of time. Trips to the bank in New Delhi and the stress of not having money wore on me. During this period of turmoil, I became sick. I tried to stay with the group but the stress related sickness wore on me and my attitude and outlook became dark and negative. I needed to get away from the crowd.

I moved into an Indian family's house in the town of Mehrali. I met the family the previous year while staying at the monastery. The father offered me a place to stay to recover. The other four friends who did not lose their money in the robbery took Peter and Yvonne under their wing. A week passed and the bank still delayed the return of my checks. The group of six headed off to Nepal promising to keep in touch.

I took several weeks to recover. When I finally did get back on my feet I knew it was no accident Yvonne, Peter and I separated paths. I wanted to explore meditation at a deeper level. Touring the subcontinent of India with Peter and Yvonne did not allow the time to fulfill my desire. They would be traveling with others exploring India for the first time. I did receive a letter from Yvonne in Nepal and she appeared to be fine. I also heard Peter became involved in meditation somewhere in the south of India and gave up his astrological practice.

India is a country of mystery. It seems to direct those who are seeking inner guidance to whatever form they need to complete this journey. I do not know how it works but I do know that those who came to find inner peace through meditation found it in some practice. I seemed to be on the verge of finding direction in my search as well and I could hardly wait.

Chapter 40
Mahendra

The Indian family allowing me into their home did so with open arms. Six boys and one girl made up the children population. All the kids except the oldest, Paul, went to school. Paul managed the family export business selling wholesale Indian clothing to westerners. The goods were shipped to the country where the western traveler lived. They were then sold either to stores or retailed in markets. Many westerners knew about the family and bought clothing items or dropped by to visit and drink tea.

The father, Mahendra, came from a Sikh family. He chose not to remain in the tradition of his father. He cut his hair and lived as a traditional Indian without the Sikh dress code or rituals. He did not get along with his father who lived in the same town but the children visited their grandfather all the time. I believe the grandfather owned a retail store in the community. His family was part of the exchange made when Hindus and Sikhs moved from what is now called Pakistan back to the new India. Many Muslims also made the journey but in the opposite direction. They were forced to move from India to the new country of Pakistan.

Mahendra Bhopal was the full name of the father and he controlled his family from within the walled compound of his home. He rarely went out from the enclosure and all visitors met him in his front sitting room. My stay with the Bhopal family was the beginning of an up and down relationship lasting two years. I would eventually travel to Holland helping the oldest son adjust to life in Europe. This part of the journey would not play out for another ten months. First I needed to explore the reason I returned to India.

Chapter 41
Meditation

After several weeks of recovering from my sickness I regained my strength and began helping around the house. I became the shopping servant in the household. Mahendra's wife would give me the vegetable shopping list and I would go to the market in Mehrauli. This job forced me to learn the names of the main vegetables and fruits as well as practice my Hindi in conversation with the vendors.

I stayed mostly in Mehrauli and the home of Mahendra for another month. While living in the home I got to meet and talk to the many western tourists coming by to visit and buy goods from Paul and the family business.

One day some travelers came by and started to talk about a man by the name of Goenka who taught meditation courses throughout India. The retreats took ten days to complete and the next class began in a suburb of Bombay. I told Mahendra I wanted to practice meditation and enroll into this class. I prepared for the journey and left a few days later.

Many teachers taught different types of meditation in India in the 70s. For some reason the name Goenka spoke to me. I felt drawn to this teacher before I even met him. I boarded the train to Bombay not knowing how the journey would play out. I never attended a retreat before and the unknown awaited me.

I arrived in the area of Bombay where the meditation course took place. Many followers of another teacher named Bhagwan Shree Rajneesh also traveled to the same suburb of Bombay. Bhagwan maintained an ashram nearby and taught his particular type of meditation there.

In the 70s many westerners came to India after the Beatles brought Maharishi Yoga to America and England. The search for inner truth spread throughout the West during the 70s. India held the key. There existed many paths in the east leading to the same truth. My search for the truth lay before me. I made the first step. I bought a flashlight and started looking.

The meditation course took place in an Indian hotel with sleeping rooms on the second floor. The kitchen and eating hall remained on the first floor including a large room for group meditation. All the rooms surrounded a courtyard in the middle of the hotel. The cooking and meal preparation lay in the skilled hands of older students. All of the kitchen help were experienced in the practice of meditation and they offered their services as a gift to the new students. Our rooms in which we slept consisted of a bedroll on the floor. Students needed to bring their own blankets. A meditation hall was set up in a big room downstairs.

As I walked past the large hall used for meditation I noticed some people already practicing. I brought a cushion with me to use during the ten-day course. I observed pads and pillows marking the spots of other students. The early claiming of territory emphasized the student's silent statement,

"This is where I am for the next ten days."

I placed my cushion against a wall. I held a strong concern regarding an old lower back problem. The physical annoyance saved me from going to Vietnam. Would the same physical handicap hold up during the hour meditation sittings practiced throughout the day and evening? The wall in the rear of the hall would be my crutch.

Americans made up the largest population attending this course. The remainder of young adults included French and Germans. The three main meditation sittings incorporated one in the early morning after breakfast. Another took place before lunch and the last one in the evening. The three group meditation sessions included S.N. Goenka. In the evening after the hour-long sitting a dharma talk by Goenka took place just before going to bed around 9 p.m.

The first sitting on day one happened in the afternoon after lunch. The first three days of the course consisted of a concentration practice. We would watch our breath go in and out of our nose. This technique called Anapana helped to focus the mind. Included in the practice of watching our breath was the holding of one's body in an upright position without moving. This completed the torture rules for the next few days.

I believe a large percentage of people practicing meditation remember the first time they actually sat. I experienced some excitement and at the same time nervousness. Sitting in a cross leg position for an hour without moving loomed before me as a huge undertaking and challenge.

My only instruction at the first sitting session was to become aware of my breath going in and going out my nose. Thoughts would arise and I needed only to observe them until they eventually dissipated. As my mind became more calm I might experience some feelings on my upper lip. Whatever happened I needed only to observe. If the feelings presented as good, observe. If an uncomfortable throbbing arises, only observe. This is the practice, non-attachment, and observation.

After ten minutes of sitting the sensations in different parts of my body started to manifest. My lower back began to ache. My knees throbbed and I no longer could watch any breath go in and out of my nose.

"I have to do this for ten days?" were the thoughts that filled my head.

The fear of not being able to make it through an hour let alone ten days overwhelmed me. I leaned back against the wall for support to help relieve the stabbing pain in the lower spine. I did my best to return to the practice of observing the breath. My awareness of my nose lost all importance. Getting to the end of the hour dominated the total process.

The concentration or Anapana part of the meditation lasted three days. Each student approached either Goenka or a meditation assistant to discuss any concerns regarding the practice. We also meditated together for a few minutes with the instructors and then return to our sitting locations.

I do not think I mentioned any concerns to the instructors other than my body aching in several places and my mind not wanting to stay with the breathing for long periods. I experienced the exact problems other new meditation students admitted to. We were told to keep trying. Always return to the breath and increase focus as long as we could.

By the third day the torture chamber loosening its' grip on me. The periods of time spent observing the breath became longer and the physical discomforts started to lessen. My back still needed the support of the wall but I slowly adjusted to the routine. I no longer counted each minute as one moment closer to the end of the ten-day course.

During the first evening talk, Goenka told of his journey when he took his first Vipassana meditation course. He became a wealthy Indian businessman after growing up in Burma where he was born. Eventually, he developed migraine headaches and traveled the world looking for a cure. Becoming addicted to morphine appeared to be his only answer to the affliction. None of the doctors in the world could help him.

One day a friend told Goenka of a Burmese man who taught Vipassana meditation. The practice of meditation could be a remedy for his terrible condition.

Goenka told the meditation students of the doubts he experienced and how he almost left the retreat. He heard no bells and felt no wonderful sensations his fellow meditation students talked about. As a final move, he instructed his car driver to wait outside the compound to help him in his escape.

Before Goenka completed his exit he was told by his teacher, U Ba Khin, not to be distracted by what other students were experiencing. He only needed to concentrate on his own breathing. When bell sounds were heard he was to only observe them. When wonderful sensations arose only observe them. Painful sensations are treated the same. Observe only.

"Do not become trapped by desire or aversion. Remain in the moment of what is happening. It is here, in this place of the present, all suffering falls away and one is free."

These words kept Goenka in the retreat. He finished the course and made meditation a part of his life. He mastered the practice and went on to teach this technique to hundreds of thousands of people from all around the world. Today there are Vipassana meditation centers everywhere. Sites can be found using the web and typing in Goenka.

The preceding narrative is the short version of the Goenka story. I remained in my first retreat and the pain in my knees and lower back still throbbed. Five more days left. On day seven I decided to do the next sitting without leaning back against the wall for relief and support.

The last part of the meditation directed the students to pass their concentrated mind through their bodies, observing the sensations throughout. Sweeping the observing mind through my back area remained a difficult task. I kept being drawn to the region of the lumbar due to the amount of throbbing pain. I set my intention to only observe the sensations in the area of discomfort and not try to force anything to happen. Non-attached observation.

After a couple of minutes, while watching the pain, something happened. An energy rush passed up my spine and the tight area in my back released. The region of discomfort compared to four or five rope knots tied by a boy scout earning his first class badge. Suddenly the bindings untied and the rope straightened. Energy shot up my spine in a sudden rush. I never felt anything like this ever before.

After the meditation session finished I no longer needed to sit against a wall for back support. I moved my sitting pillow towards the middle of the room. I had released an area in my body from a possible lifetime of pain.

Completing the first ten days course I signed up for a second one beginning in the afternoon. I finished the second retreat and decided to make meditation a part of my life. Meditation is a practice. Being a member of one religion or another is not necessary. Even though Vipassana is a technique taught by Buddhists one does not have to be a Buddhist to practice Vipassana. Vipassana meditation became a turning point in my life and I even practice it today, forty years later.

I completed the second course and headed back to Delhi and the Mahendra family. I stayed with them for several more months, practicing meditation in the mornings and evenings and shopping for fruit and vegetables during the day. I needed to make the practice a part of my daily routine and living with the family allowed this to happen.

I became a friend with the oldest son Paul. He seemed to do all the work regarding the family business. The father would be the social contact with the westerners coming to his door. The second son would do odd jobs for the family. I do not think son number two received any training to work in the family business. If number two grew up in Europe he might have been given instruction in the field of a trade or technical skill. Higher education held no interest for him.

I discovered a fact about the Indian family pecking order while living with Mahendra. The father is the boss. Son number one is next in line. He expects and gets obedience from all his younger brothers without question. The second son was a large young man and physically he could have challenged Paul. Within the Indian hierarchy, such an attempt would never happen.

Paul bossed his younger brother around like a servant and number two responded without question.

Being the first-born is a big deal in the east. In the west, such a pecking order does not exist. I could only boss my two younger brothers around until physical size bridged the gap. My youngest brother is now bigger than both his older brothers. This really sucks.

Chapter 42
Escaping the Heat in India

Christmas and the month of December passed without much fanfare. I now lived in a country without many Christians so the shopping frenzy of gifts and celebration could not be found. I did some traveling during the next few months. The Taj Mahal and other places of interest are all within a short train ride from New Delhi. Winters in northern India can be cool. The local population wears warm wraps to protect themselves from the winter blasts coming down from the Himalayas. The cool conditions last a few months. By the end of February, the worst of the cold no longer held a grip on the New Delhi region of northern India.

With March the first signs of spring emerge. The warm weather clothing fashions paraded around town by wealthy young Indian women start to appear. The newest colors and patterns in Saris strut along the streets of New Delhi. Saris show off well against the smooth brown skin of Indian women. Soon the months of June and July would arrive. Along with high temperatures comes the Monsoon season.

When the British ruled India the wealthy families of the military officers and government officials went to the foothills of the Himalayan Mountains and stayed for the summer. They would wait out the heat and pouring rains of the lowlands in the towns located at 6000 ft or higher. The lower ranked lieutenants took over the command posts for their superiors during the next few months. With only a fan moving the hot air around in an attempt to keep cool the summer in the lowlands remained a challenge to survive. Promotion to a higher rank allowed the career officers to join the privileged few in the high elevation towns like Darjeeling and the Kulu Valley during this warm season.

Mention of the Monsoon rains should also be given when talking about Indian summers. I live in Arizona at the time of this writing where the desert heat also attracts a rainy season called the Monsoon. The reader should not mix the two because they hold little in common. The desert rains in Arizona are the result of intense thunderstorms sweeping over the valley of the sun and dropping moisture in isolated areas. The rains can be intense and may include car damaging hail and intense winds. Flash flooding may occur but usually, the heavy rain is short lived.

The Monsoon in India is also brought on by heat rising up and out of the northern plains of India. The land heats up faster than the oceans in the Bay of Bengal or Arabian Sea so a low-pressure system develops over the plains of India sucking in the moisture from these nearby oceans. The amount of moisture can be vast and flooding usually occurs. India depends on the yearly rains for the growing of rice and other crops using copious amounts of water.

I happened to be in New Delhi during one such Monsoon rain in July. To experience such rains in this part of the world belittles the attempt of Arizona in naming their rainy season the Monsoon. Rain in Arizona comes in drops of moisture. We call them raindrops. Rain in India arrives in buckets. There are no raindrops. Only a continuous dumping of water without the separation between droplets pours from the sky. Umbrellas serve little purpose. Most Indians prefer to seek cover when the torrent begins. Some dance in the streets in a ritual display performed by the younger population as they show their bravery standing up to the watery blasts from the heavens. Streets become flooded in minutes. I observed a four-foot deep river flowing past the Mahendra house covering an unlucky car parked in the low part of the street. If India sells flood insurance the purchase would be a smart investment.

By May the heat brought the temperatures back to levels of discomfort. I choose to be among the privileged few who swarmed to the cool weather of the hillside villages. I said goodbye to Mahendra and his family and started the journey to the town of Manali, above the Kulu Valley.

When you travel to mountain towns the trains reach only the base of the peaks. From the last train stop the traveler switches to either a car or a bus in order to travel up the steep windy road. Manali is located at the west end of the foothills. Before traveling to this hill community I heard a story by another traveler. The tale turned out to be not only an interesting one but also true.

Alexander the Great reached India in 326 B.C. during his world conquest attempt but died soon after making his presence known. Alexander's desire to march to the end of the world may have been a grand vision but his troops did not share the same view. A mutiny by his warriors, while in India, forced Alexander to give up his dream. He died soon after while retreating back to his home.

The story, shared by other travelers, told of a number of Alexander's men not wanting to make the long trip back to Macedonia. Many decided to stay in India. The tale explained how the men married local women in the area and began a mini culture including sheep herding and weaving of wool products. These skills were the traditions of their homeland.

The area where the remnants of Alexander's army lived today was located half way up the road to the Kulu Valley. I kept my eyes open while riding in the bus up the long mountain pass. All of a sudden history appeared in front of me. A flock of sheep started across the road and forced the bus to stop. The men herding the sheep were dressed in Greek-style tunics and hats. I knew the style of the clothing because I saw such outfits during ceremonial holidays when I stayed in Greece.

When Greeks dressed up in their old traditional costumes during festivals the style matched exactly what these men were wearing. Nowhere else in India or any other eastern culture does a known Macedonian ancestry exist. They are still there. If you ever have a chance to take a bus ride to Kulu, keep your eyes open. History may cross your path. It did mine and I remained in awe of having witnessed the remains of a Greek army family tree, thousands of miles from its' homeland.

Chapter 43
Manali

Manali is a small mountain town located at an elevation of around 8,000 ft. There are two main crops grown in this high elevation hillside community, apples, and ganja. The second crop is the reason why hundreds of western hippies and Indian Sadhus converge onto the settlement every summer.

I got off the bus. The town plaza contained chillum (pipe) smoking westerners and a few Indian holy men. If music was added the gathering could be compared to a miniature Woodstock. They all came to Manali for the same reasons the British officers did before them. All wanted to escape the lowland heat and summer rains. The cool nights and temperate days compared the hill station to Flagstaff, Arizona, the town I lived in for ten years and where I wrote this book.

A couple of Americans approached me in the square. I began to look for a place to stay and again the Universe gave me what I asked for. The two young men needed people to join them in a large house they rented in the middle of an apple orchard. I grabbed my backpack and set out through the woods to the farm structure located twenty minutes from town.

The house was surrounded by apple trees and meadows and stood alone away from any neighbor dwellings. I needed a quiet place to practice meditation and the farm structure met my requirements. The second floor contained four separate rooms for individuals to sleep. A long hallway proceeded to a kitchen area where portable stoves cooked the meals. I rented a small nook at the end of the hall. The room contained windows on two walls so plenty of sunlight greeted me each morning.

I came to the mountain town to practice meditation and avoid the blistering heat of the Indian lowland summers. The other housemates journeyed here for the summer harvest still months away. Their enterprise included buying Indian artifacts and filling them with hash they harvested. The statues were then sent to friends back home. The hash business enabled the group to stay in India and continue the lifestyle of living well and staying high.

After several weeks the household changed. Three of the westerners needed to return to the Indian lowland for business and they indicated they might be gone for several months. The fourth partner remained with me. We knew the rent for only two would be a lot. I went into the town and waited for the bus to arrive bringing more westerners out of the heat of the lowlands.

A young woman from Germany named Marva, Robert from England and a couple from the states decided to join us in our apple house retreat. All the rooms were now full and the rent became manageable. While living together we decided to make the chore of cooking a group effort. We took turns creating dinner for everyone but we were on our own for breakfast and lunch. This schedule worked out well.

Robert, a young man from England, just arrived in India. The excitement of being in this fascinating mountain village filled his adventurous spirit. Marva lived in India for a while and just left a relationship. She tried to have a baby several months before but experienced a miscarriage. Her ex-partner's name was Avram, Marva spelled backward. I never knew their given birth names. Avram remained in an ashram where he stayed with his guru practicing meditation.

The two Americans met in India and were still working out their relationship. The young man seemed possessive of his girlfriend and did not trust her being anywhere without him. The woman had learned meditation from a Rajneesh retreat months before and many mornings we would wake up to her practice of chanting,

"Who, Who, Who"

The words are a part of the ritual. The person chanting is asking the universe,

"Who am I?"

I cannot elaborate on the practice because I never attended a retreat conducted by Rajneesh. The only comment I feel qualified to make about the different spiritual practices in the world is this. If you find one and it feels good then stick with it. My teacher, Goenka, always told students during the courses he taught not to mix different practices. He compared such an attempt of combining different meditations to standing with one foot in one canoe and the other foot in another canoe. Make a mental picture in your mind of doing such a physical feat and you can understand how dangerous such an effort might be.

Life in Manali went by fairly smoothly. Our family of boarders in the farmhouse carried out the different duties needed to keep the household together. I rose every morning at sunrise to meditate and watch my breath. The sound of chanting by the Rajneesh follower would sometimes break the morning silence. Breakfast happened on our own and whoever cooked dinner in the evening had to make a run to town for fresh vegetables.

One evening as I sat outside the rented farmhouse surrounded by apple trees and contemplating life, I witnessed something I have never seen before. I did a lot of reflection while in my 20s and I felt meditation helped slow my mind down and provide a space for 'me time'. The evening remained in the period of dusk and the surrounding pine trees near the farm were still visible in dark shadow form.

Off to my right, I noticed some movement along the ground. It appeared to be a squirrel running from rock to rock and stopping long enough to catch its' breath. It stayed just ahead of another squirrel following close behind. The first animal seemed to be baiting the second one into keeping one step away from catching up. Just as the second tree climber reached the first one, the first squirrel would scamper off quickly repeating the game over and over again. Eventually, the open area where the chase played out reached a group of tall pines and the leader of the game scurried up the sixty-foot giant. It stopped only to tease its' pursuer into following. I thought to myself,

"What will the squirrel do when it reaches the top? There is nowhere else to go."

Ten seconds later I received my answer. The first squirrel leaped from the top of the tree into open space just as the second one arrived at the apex of the pine. As it leaped the front paws spread out to the sides as well as the back feet forming a spread eagle approach to the animal's dive. Between the front and back appendages hung a sheet of skin now serving as a brace against the wind formed by the squirrel's freefall into the evening's air. Instead of a direct drop to the ground, the usual direction an object would take after plunging from a sixty-foot pine tree, the squirrel glided across the evening sky at an angle almost horizontal allowing it to drop from the great height at a speed similar to a parachute skydiver just before landing. Within seconds the pursuer made its' leap into the darkening sky and the two 'Rocky' squirrels gently dropped to the ground safe and full of energy as they continued to play their chase game into the night.

I had just witnessed flying squirrels for the first and only time in my life. I did not know they existed in India and the shock of seeing these gliding nut gatherers in person stunned me for a few minutes as I reflected on my thoughts about the evening's performance. India can do that. Just when you think you have seen it all another act presents itself and the universe has another good laugh after giving you such a gift.

During the three months spent in Manali, Marva met a Holy man in the next town down the valley. The guru went to the West to teach his style of meditation. He returned and brought several westerners with him to practice his techniques. His home became an ashram for westerners to come and meditate. He housed several followers on the day we went for a visit and they seemed devoted to him and his teachings.

While on our pilgrimage to his home Marva invited him to our apple orchard abode in Manali. He came several days later and talked about different spiritual matters and drank tea with us. During the visit, Marva slipped some LSD into his drink and did not tell him what she did until he started to leave to catch the bus home. He seemed fine with the hallucination drug in his system. His ride on the bus must have been different. Marva seemed to be the kind of person who slipped unknown drugs into your drink so you needed to be careful around her, especially at tea time.

Another person who came into our circle of friends lived in India for several years. Her Indian name was Pavitra, which meant purity. Her English name was Patricia. If you own an English passport you can stay in India as long as you like. India remained indebted for the railroad, language, and political systems the Limeys left behind.

Pavitra taught in a girl's school for a year soon after her arrival in India. She also traveled to the far east of India to the state of Assam with another friend named Greg. Being Australian he too held a timeless access to India and any country previously under British rule. People owning a British or Australian passport had the advantage of living in any country still in the British Commonwealth.

In 1973 Assam existed as an isolated state. The population lived under tribal laws instead of Indian government rule. Stories circulated about life in the more primitive areas where the practice of head hunting still existed. Taking a head helped to control population growth among the tribes. No wonder the Indian government made Assam a restricted area. A few missionaries from England may have tried to spread their faith in these isolated regions and ended up shorter by 10 to 12 inches. This measurement would depend on the size of the religious leader's head.

Pavitra and I became friends and decided to travel together. Greg introduced us to another Australian couple named Ray and Deborah. At the time of our meeting I had no idea I would be involved with this couple in their Australian homeland from 1976 to 1979.

Pavitra and I soon headed back to the West. She needed to visit her mother and I needed to return to Europe. My visa expired four months before and the Indian government did not give me an extension. During the Pakistan, Indian war the U.S. sided with Pakistan and the Indian government held little love for Americans in their country.

Before leaving Manali I experienced one more interesting story worth passing on. I can only give details as to what I saw and ensure the reader the event really happened.

I started making plans to leave Manali and continue on to Dalhousie, another hill station in the western foothills of India. I planned to attend another meditation course taught by Goenka.

The hashish season started a week before my departure date and the countryside became increasingly inundated by hash harvesting hippies from the west. I mentioned before apples and hash or ganja remained the two crops produced in the mountain valley town. While sitting in a restaurant in town with a few friends a local Indian came up to us and offered to sell some of the new hash he just processed. The making of hash in this Indian community is a primitive and painstaking task. The plants grow wild throughout the fields of the countryside. The pot plants are allowed to go to seed so there will be another crop the following year.

When the plants are ready an oily, sticky film covers them. The harvester simply rubs the plant in an upward motion making sure he does not damage the plant. The marijuana will continue to produce this sticky substance containing the THC. The THC is the drug in the plant giving the user the high.

The sticky substance collects onto the hands of the harvester like a thin layer of glue or film of dirt. The harvester begins to rub his hands together back and forth. Small pellets of dark, sticky dirt-like clay begin to form on his hands. By collecting the small pellets of hash and packing them into a larger ball the harvester can put the sphere of pure hash into a container and continue on to the next plant.

My hash-harvesting roommates told me an experienced harvester needed a day to collect a wad of hash the size of a small ping-pong ball. I came to Manali to watch my breath and indulge in the practice of meditation so I never joined in with the farmers of this crop.

The harvester in the restaurant just finished rubbing the hash from his hands hours before and offered some to try before one made a purchase. I separated myself from smoking these Indian products and did so for the whole summer. The harvester took apart a cigarette, mixed the hash in the tobacco, re-rolled it, lit it and passed it around the table. I decided this would be my going away party so I joined in.

I think the rolled joint made it around the table twice and lucky for us only twice. Freshly rubbed hash straight from the field contained the most potent level of THC I ever experienced.

While sitting in the booth I soon realized I no longer possessed the ability to talk or communicate. The others in the group seemed fine. I really could not do much more than nod my head, drink tea and look at the surroundings in the restaurant and market just outside the door. Everything vibrated in a manner I never before experienced.

While in this state, I could see energy waves coming out of people and animals. As I sat in the booth I noticed a dog from across the street. I knew the dog from my previous trips into town. He belonged to one of the Indian vendors at the vegetable market. At this moment in time the experience of seeing Rover opened me to something I had never seen before or since this day.

The canine demonstrated something was wrong. His body shook all over as he stood in one spot. All of a sudden he stiffened and nothing moved. In the same moment, I saw a small cloud looking like a field of light or energy leave his body and dissipate into the air. As soon as the force field vanished the body of the dog fell over to the side. The dog remained as stiff as a piece of wood. When it fell over the carcass collapsed as one unit. It is my belief I witnessed the energy life force of the dog leave its' body at the moment of death.

I don't know if I would have witnessed the event without the induced mind altering hash affecting my perception. I watched the owner discover the dead dog. He picked him up and carried him away.

Communication continued to escape me for several hours. Soon the effects of the hash wore off and the ability of speech returned. I asked my friends if they noticed the dying dog. None witnessed the death of this canine. The experience remained mine alone.

I stopped contemplating the incident for many years. I doubt I would have any interest from listeners in the West. Many would not believe me so I never repeated the story before writing this book. I said at the beginning I possess no explanation for the event. I can only report what I witnessed.

I think the moment presented itself for a quote I came across while traveling. The above event is a perfect example of the following passage.

"He who travels far will often see things far removed from what he believes was truth. When he talks about it in the fields at home, he is often accused of lying, for the obdurate people will not believe what they do not see and distinctly feel. Inexperience, I believe, will give little credence to my song." (Believed to be a quote by Hermann Hesse)

Chapter 44
Return to Europe

The day for leaving Manali had arrived. Marva and the Englishman, Robert, left the morning before to go to the valley. Both of them needed to arrange their travel itinerary. Pavitra and I took the bus to Dalhousie to attend the next ten-day meditation course before heading west. The class came at a good time for me to strengthen the practice of Vipassana. I also needed the time to heal from dysentery I picked up right before I left Manali. My healing consisted of the Indian medicines purchased at any pharmacy and a change of diet. Dysentery became a common sickness for westerners traveling in India and the Rx stores shelved many types of remedies.

The ten-day course returned many of the meditation students I met in Bombay months before. I do not know where they spent their warm summer months. I crossed paths with a few French students in Manali but no other Americans from Bombay stayed there. The hash population of the Kulu Valley probably did not mix well with the spiritual seekers of the west.

After practicing meditation in Dalhousie Pavitra and I returned to Mahendra's house to finish up some last minute business. Paul left for Holland weeks before and he now lived with friends in Amsterdam. Paul flew there to set up a business in clothing for the family. Mahendra wanted me to follow him and help him get started. Pavitra flew to England shortly after we arrived in Delhi. We promised to keep in touch.

Before going to Manali I sent for the remaining $4000 my grandfather willed me. I told Mahendra I wanted him to use $3000 of the check to help westerners stranded in India to get back to the West. Many such travelers were in India and I thought this would be a good use for the money. I wanted Mahendra to hold $1000 for me to use when I needed it. I become a part of the family after living there for several months. I promised to help Paul get settled in Amsterdam and establish some business ties.

I flew from Delhi to Paris on a flight passing through a wealthy Arab oil country by the name of United Arab Emirates. The plane left New Delhi and landed in the capital of Dubai. Passengers traveling on to Europe needed to change planes. Those traveling west were allowed to walk around the terminal at Dubai. In the airport I saw what oil wealth brought to this desert land. The airport was both modern, well maintained, and sold items in the gift shops of high quality and price. I doubted if a middle or lower class existed amongst this wealthy Arab country. I remained the only passenger wearing western clothing. All the people in the terminal wore the styles of robes and headscarves typical of Dubai and other Arab countries.

After many more hours of flight from Dubai, the plane landed in Paris. I caught the bus into town and got off at the main station where I boarded the train to Amsterdam. I stayed for ten months in India and my system seemed to be in shock after returning to Europe hours of having just left India. I appeared to the public as a little intense. My long hair, mustache and Indian homespun pants and shirt did not fit in with the styles on the streets of Paris or Europe.

On the train, I shared a passenger cabin with a group of young teenage schoolgirls in their uniforms and matching shoes. They must have been on a school outing to some place of educational interest. The sight of me became one of intense speculation and awe.

I smoked at this time in my life. The Indian cigarette called a Beedie looked as different as the smells it produced. The hand rolled smoke is made from a plant different than tobacco so the two combined to create talk and speculation among the girls. They must have thought I was doing something illegal right there on the train.

After a while, a few of them got the courage to try their English on me. This lasted until the head teacher came to my rescue and gave instructions in French scattering them back to their seats. She probably told them something like,

"This is what happens to you when you don't do well in school and don't meet and marry the right man."

Young girls seem to be attracted to the bizarre and totally different. They probably wanted to experience more of the world before growing up and became locked into the role society planned for them. There exists a bit of the wild side in most of us. Some explore it and others do what their parents tell them. Talking to me on the train showed some of the young girl's desire to discover their own wild side.

Chapter 45
Amsterdam 1973 to 1974

One of the many canals found throughout Amsterdam.

I arrived in Amsterdam and eventually found the address where Paul lived. The couple living in the apartment with Paul also knew the Mahendra family. The small space contained one bedroom so Paul slept on the floor in the living room. Paul arrived in Holland a month before and still displayed culture shock. His only contact with other Westerners before coming to Europe were the ones stopping by his home in India. These travelers usually dressed in the clothing of India and numbered two or three at a time.

The modern homes, roads, and shopping in Holland could not be compared to anything he experienced in India. Stores gave each shopper a plastic bag after a purchase. In India, plastic bags were considered a luxury and few stores gave them out for free. By the time I arrived Paul managed to save about forty such bags to send to his mother back in India. The wealth of the West to a young Indian boy of twenty years in 1973 was overwhelming.

A Red Light district exists in Amsterdam where the women display themselves in the windows as a major attraction to tourists from all over the world. A traveler can even do the wine and cheese boat trip up the canals surrounding the district so they do not have to mingle with all the men from Arab nations taking full advantage of this attraction. Paul, probably still a virgin, may have been waiting for his family to arrange his wedding back in India. The openness of sex in Amsterdam also became an overload for a young man from India and Paul needed time to adjust.

A day after I arrived the couple moved Paul and me to the home of a friend who owned a much larger apartment. We stayed in the bigger abode for several weeks while looking for a more permanent place. Paul remained in my care now and these friends of the Mahendra family no longer wanted to help with Paul's adjustment in the West.

Eventually, we found something called a 'cracked house'. This is not a drug related term but something different. The law in Amsterdam allowed people to stay in rooms of a building if the structure is empty. The homes or offices may be on a list for remodeling work but many months may exist before the work is scheduled. The law served several purposes. Empty buildings are exposed to vandals and junkies crashing in them. If you allow students or none drug users to stay in the building for a small fee they will keep an eye on it while it is waiting to be either sold or renovated. Rent is collected and the inhabitants have a place to live at a reasonable price.

We found such a building on Keizersgracht in the heart of the city. We moved into the small bedroom with the bathroom down the hall. Paul and I slept there at night and worked in the day. We considered ourselves lucky. A good place to live in the middle of the city for low rent is a real find. I maintained a positive perspective and at the same time felt some power continuing to look after me. Some people call the sense of being watched over their guardian angel. I did not give the feeling a name, I just remained grateful for being guided to the perfect spot.

Paul also possessed several boxes of Indian clothing he was trying to sell to local stores. The problem facing Paul stemmed from the fact his family back in India owned a great deal of Indian clothing no longer in style. Paul needed to try and sell the items to stores. I could see the Mahendra family knew little about which clothing items were popular in Europe. Their belief centered on the idea that Paul only needed to get to Holland because everyone would buy the clothing and the family would be rich. This false reasoning was now crumbling under the wall of reality.

The summer season drew to a close. Indian clothing sold better in the warm weather. Paul and I managed to sell a few of the handicraft lines still popular with the public. For the next five months, we would have to do our best to survive. I got to know a few of the inhabitants of the building and spent many nights talking with them and learning about the Dutch culture. Paul met a single woman who practiced law in Amsterdam and spent a lot of time with her.

I found the Dutch the most open and friendly people I met in Europe. Even though I only stayed in Amsterdam for a year I still reflect back to how close I came to making the city my home. The Dutch learn several languages in school. English is the second language and is spoken the most throughout the country.

The Dutch maintain an open mind about many things illegal in most of Europe. On the Queen's birthday people are allowed freedoms to do things not permitted on the other 364 days of the year. Whatever they do cannot involve hurting other citizens. During the yearly parade for the Queen, the smell of hash fills the air and the police are only present to prevent any physical conflicts.

There are a lot of drugs available in Holland. I witnessed several young people destroy their lives trying heroine and becoming addicted. I am sure I would find this to be true in most major cities throughout the world. Despite the large amount of drugs, Amsterdam is the one European city I would live in if given the chance again.

During the winter months, I spent several evenings each week going to a place called Cosmos. The Dutch built three clubs in Amsterdam catering to young people between the ages of 18 and 30. I especially liked this club because they offered meditation classes, eastern music, a health food restaurant, and a mixed-use sauna. The Cosmos maintained a positive atmosphere allowing a new member to meet other people in a welcoming space. I continued my practice of meditation at the club and found myself around people interested in the same spiritual and healthy lifestyles as myself.

I visited one of the other clubs once and found a completely different atmosphere. Walking into the building the first thing offered to the member included a range of hash sticks from all over the world. Hash could be sold in private clubs as long as those indulging smoked the drug in the club. The atmosphere attracted a type of person who'd rather get wasted on something and sit for the rest of the evening sipping on tea and listening to Mick Jagger and other heavy rock bands during the mid-70s era. The club's atmosphere compared to the same heavy energy of the morphine junkies in India the night the German Sadhu arrived at the Buddhist monastery near Mehrauli. I chose to be around the positive life force. The dark side felt too intense.

Paul still needed time to adjust to the West. A place like Cosmos did not appeal to him. He spent most of his evenings with the Dutch lawyer and he eventually moved in with her. I spent more time with the three young Dutch women whom I befriended while living on Keizersgracht, a street in Amsterdam. The nightclub remained my outlet for meditation and eastern food.

Somehow I survived the winter. In drinking bars, I sold pictures mounted on chipboard for two guilders each. I also worked in a boutique for a Dutch man who made his money selling trinkets and clothing in one of the many street markets found throughout Amsterdam. By spring I needed to find a real job and create some income.

Good fortune came my way in March. Paul managed to get his hands on an address book from some young merchants who were clothing wholesalers. The names and addresses of stores throughout Holland selling Indian clothing and goods were listed in the book. Paul copied the addresses before returning the journal to its' rightful owner. He gave me a copy as well.

By spring Paul and I parted ways. For a few months after leaving the Keizersgracht address, we move into the building Paul rented to store the clothing from India. The terms of the lease did not include the renters living there. We were soon discovered and asked to leave. Paul moved in with his Dutch lawyer girlfriend. At the same time, I received a check from my mother to cover the last three years of birthdays and Christmas presents. The date was 1974 and the time abroad now added up to three and a half years.

Amsterdam became a stable address for me for a whole year and I think my mother felt I might need the money. This check allowed me to find a comfortable apartment on Keizersstraat, a street between Keizersgracht and Herrengracht.

My time in Amsterdam amounted to almost a year. The best way to describe the country can be related to the weather of this North Sea land. I call this story,

"Where's The Sunshine?"

The event happened in the early summer of 1974. Amsterdam can have warm summers or cold summers weather wise. In 1974 the summer weather presented as cold. The days remained overcast due to the cloud cover and location near the ocean.

One day the sun came out and all of Amsterdam went into an occult worshiping ritual like I have never seen before. Long sleeve shirts and sweaters came off. Tank tops and shorts appeared from clothing chests labeled,

"Do not open unless the sun is shining."

People called in sick for work. Owners needed to either run their own businesses or join in with the movement sweeping the city.

As I walked along the canals snaking through this magnificent, postcard-perfect City the population started preparing for their worship of the sun. Deck chairs came out of storage and were placed around tables. All the boathouses lining the canals or sidewalks with access to the sun contained furniture not found the day before. Bathing suits packed until today were now in full use. Beer and drinks came out of refrigerators along with an abundance of the staple food of the Dutch. Bread and cheese. Music filled the air on every block. English tunes, as well as a few Dutch songs, poured out into the sunny afternoon. The party was about to begin.

In Amsterdam, you do not need to know how to speak Dutch or know the people in order to join in on the festival. I tried to learn Dutch for a few weeks when I first arrived but gave up. I found out carpenters and common laborers spoke better English and at a level higher than I could ever hope to learn from the Dutch classes. All I needed to do in order to join a group was to say hi and share where I came from and why I chose to live in Amsterdam. The Dutch are some of the

most friendly, liberal minded people in the world and they are the most accepting of different cultures and beliefs of any nation I have come across. Now you see why I almost lived there.

The day continued with the Sunshine cult staying in the warmth until the sun set in the west below the British Isles. The next day we all awoke to the cloud covered skies. Overcast seemed to be the norm for Amsterdam this summer. Everyone went back to work and employers forgave the lame excuses of their employees. They knew sun worshiping played a part of what to expect in Amsterdam when the sun came out. The party shut down for the moment and the summer clothing was carefully placed back into the trunks marked 'Do not open unless the sun is shining'. Everyone held the hope they would again see the solar sphere called "the sun" before the month of October.

In the evening I went into a pub to get a beer and be around the Dutch who all survived one of the most magnificent citywide parties I ever witnessed. After about an hour of being in the pub, I heard a voice yell loudly above the noise level of the bar.

"Isn't that interesting," he screamed in English, "summer came on a Tuesday this year."

The laughter following the declaration came with a few groans of recognition. The comment could easily be true. I realized warm weather and sunny skies may not be a part of the normal summer patterns. If I wanted to live in this special part of Europe I needed to accept this fact. "The sun doesn't shine very much."

Soon after moving into the apartment on Herenstraat, Pavitra arrived in Holland.

She had been visiting her family in England and Spain. Her mother had moved to Spain to be near her oldest daughter. This move allowed her pension to go further. Living in Spain in the 70s provided many retirees from England more purchasing ability and a more comfortable life.

By the time Pavitra arrived I already started a clothing wholesale business using the addresses I received from Paul. The Dutchman, Mark, who owned the boutique where I worked gave me his van to use three days of the week. I sold his extra stock of clothing and a few items from some other Dutch friends. Pavitra worked with me and by summer we ran a thriving wholesale business throughout Holland.

The two main reasons I believe our traveling wholesale business worked are as follows: Pavitra and I traveled to the locations of the shops selling the wares. The door-to-door service eliminated the boutique owners from traveling to Amsterdam and buying from the import stores. The second reason we did so well was because of the current styles we sold. We did not sell clothing in fashion the year before. We sold the trendy skirts and blouses women wanted.

One store in Zeeland located in the south of Holland could not wait for our three-week return. I needed to send by mail a box of skirts to the owner because the women in the town purchased all of the items we sold to him after four days.

By the end of summer the money filled our bank account. Mark made a lot of money as well but he hid his wealth in his sock drawer so he would not pay taxes on all he earned. Mark expressed interest in expanding his worth by having me become his wholesaler. He knew Pavitra and I wanted to return to India. Mark created a few designs of blouses and skirts and gave me a wad of money hoping all would work out.

By September Pavitra and I prepared to fly to India and eventually on to Australia. Her friends, Greg, Ray, and Deborah were still trying to buy land in Australia and move to the country. Pavitra was determined to be a part of the move. I felt neutral about the country lifestyle but I was willing to try it out.

I returned to Amsterdam in 2008 on my way to Italy with my present wife, Suzanne. Thirty-five years passed since I lived there in Holland. I tried to find the apartment where I stayed on Herrenstraat. Over the years many of the businesses changed on the street. I think I narrowed the apartment where I lived down to two possibilities. The bakery on the same street became a trendy coffee house with rolls and other pastries made in the back of the store. Different businesses operated along the street but a change came to them as well over the years. Different paint colors altered any markers I may have remembered but the neighborhood still existed as a beautiful street in the heart of Amsterdam.

Giving the reader a little history of Amsterdam as it is written in Wikipedia is something I could do. Instead, I suggest a traveler to take one of the many historical boat tours through the canals. You will receive a detailed accounting of how the city started, expanded and became the waterway city of today. Also look at some of the many pictures of Amsterdam provided by Google. As the saying states, "A picture is worth a thousand words."

Amsterdam remains, for me, the most beautiful city in Europe. I still think about how close I came to making Holland a permanent place to live.

Chapter 46
Back to India, 1974

Pavitra and I flew directly to New Delhi from Amsterdam. We stayed in the capital in order to complete our clothing business order. After settling in our hotel and meeting with our clothing maker, we headed to Mehrauli and a visit with Mahendra.

The visit to the Mahendra household included our bringing a sack full of plastic bags for Paul's mother. Paul collected quite a few during the past twelve months. I spent most of my time talking to her about Paul and letting her know he remained safe and happy. Mothers in India seem to hold a special place for their first-born child. She wanted to know about the woman Paul met. Paul lived with her and I am not sure how his mother felt about this arrangement. Unmarried couples living together remained a western tradition. India did not have such a practice in 1975.

One of the most noticeable changes at the Mahendra home included the construction and addition of five rooms along the back wall of the compound. Mahendra planned to turn his home into a small hotel. Without Paul to run the clothing business in India, Mahendra needed to come up with some other business to support his large family. The day we arrived the construction stopped. By now I started to figure out where the $4000 check I gave to Mahendra went.

Pavitra and I placed our energy on our clothing shipment. We contacted a tailor in Delhi and he put his workers on the order right away. We were given an amount of cash by Mark to pay for the clothes and ship them to Holland. Mark continued to keep his earnings from the street market in Amsterdam in his sock drawer. We were going to make more guilders (Dutch money) for Mark so he could add to his sock drawer. We all make choices in life as to how we want to live. Sock drawer banking was Mark's choice.

The clothing order would need about a month to complete. During the waiting period, Pavitra and I went to Nepal and Kathmandu. My return to Nepal remained a priority for me. I really wanted to see those Holy Mountains again. Upon arriving we met a couple in Kathmandu named Jack and Annie. They also meditated with Goenka and practiced the Vipassana technique. If you are going to watch your breath with other people you might as well do it using the same practice.

We all decided to rent a house outside the city of Kathmandu near the famous Buddhist temple called the Stupa of Bodnath. We set up a house, practiced meditation, visited Buddhist temples all around Kathmandu and enjoyed our month long vacation. I even pierced my ear using only a sewing needle and a bar of soap to back up the ear when the point of the needle came through. It hurt. Nepal is a calming place to stay when the hustle and bustle of India is overwhelming.

Buddhist monk in his finest robes at the monastery where he lived near Kathmandu.

While living in our rented house outside Kathmandu, we befriended a Nepalese forest ranger. His station of employment placed him near where we lived outside Kathmandu. He owned a home in the lowlands of Nepal where his wife and family lived. He invited Jack, Annie, Pavitra and myself to come and visit him in his home and go for an elephant ride in the jungle or Terai. He lived near the border of India and Nepal and not far from where the Buddha was born and lived as a boy 2500 years ago.

Near the end of our stay in Kathmandu, we made arrangements to meet Jack and Annie at the town of the ranger near the jungles of the lowlands. Pavitra and I wanted to travel west to another town said to have beautiful views of the Himalayas. The bus ride to Pokera took the whole day. The narrow roads twisted and turned around the hillsides and overlooked deep valleys. Such landscape kept the bus moving at a slow speed. We arrived in the late afternoon. We were well rewarded. The views of the Annapurna Range and the famous Fish Tail or Machhapuchhare Mountain were breathtaking.

In 1974 the town of Pokera consisted of food stalls, a few hotels, and surrounding picture postcard views. I went online to make sure I spelled the names of the mountains correctly and discovered images of Pokera in 2008 showing how the town grew in the past 35 years. Many more hotels were in place and the quality of restaurants improved from basic food stalls to comfortable eateries. Pokera now contained the comforts and lodgings needed by westerners coming to view and hike in the surrounding countryside.

After a couple of days in Pokera, we left to meet Jack and Annie. We took the bus down the windy road to the lower jungles of the Terai. We met our friends at the bus station where our ranger friend lived. The date, November of 1974, brought changes to Nepal. The old King died and the new King planned his coronation in February of 1975. All hippies needed to leave Kathmandu and all elephants in Nepal were ordered to make the trek to the capital to partake in the ceremony. The ranger told us he could not find any of these beasts of burden available. He believed all elephants in the area already started the long walk to Kathmandu in order to be in the parade honoring the new king.

On the second day at the ranger's house, while walking in the surrounding area, a Mahout and his elephant appeared on the road. Using our best sign language we managed to arrange a trip with him and his working beast for a tour through the jungle. The next day we all met and the ranger became our guide from the top of this magnificent animal.

The trip to the Terai or jungle went through fields of different kinds of grains and plants. The elephant seemed to be a constant eater. On the journey he would grab crops and bushes not caring whether he ate human grown plants or jungle growth. The local farmers did not mind the elephant taking a trunk load of food even if it came from their own field. What could they do? Several tons vs. 150 pounds would not even be close to a fair fight.

We soon left the farming area of the small town and entered the thick vegetation of the Terai. The trail in the thick bush could be easily seen but I believe we could go in any direction and the elephant would create his own trail. Elephants are like a four-legged bulldozer eating constantly and knocking down anything in their path.

Thirty minutes into the jungle the big, gray battering ram started to make an unusual noise. The growl coming from its' throat seemed like a warning to other animals in the woods. The ranger asked the Mahout why his elephant made such a noise. The Mahout laughed and said elephants always make such noises when they smell a tiger nearby. The Mahout did not seem worried. I thought a tiger would have to be stupid to take on this massive beast of burden.

Annie became worried. The thought of a tiger leaping down from a tree and taking out a tourist riding on an elephant was too much to handle. We turned around soon after the elephant started making the warning noises and headed back to the small village. Not one tiger made its' presence known and no one got hurt on the trip.

Jack and I took turns sitting on the neck of the elephant and turning him with our legs. If you wanted to go left you kicked under his left ear. Right turns mean a kick to the right ear. I believe starting and stopping were verbal commands. We didn't get a chance to do either one.

We paid the Mahout and returned to the ranger's home for one last night before heading back to India and finishing our clothing business. We thanked the ranger for all he did for us.

I have now ridden an elephant in Nepal and a camel in Afghanistan. Soon there may not be a need for either animal in the East. Trucks and other modern equipment are replacing both. The East is changing and so is the way work gets done.

Chapter 47
India, The Last Time

All four of us returned to Delhi to tie up loose ends. I met the tailor and paid for the shipment of clothing to be sent. We made one last visit to Mahendra and his family. By now I realized Mahendra used the money I gave him to build a small hotel for himself and send his oldest son to Holland. The $1000 I asked him to hold for me no longer existed. The reaction I received from him, when I asked about the money told me our friendship no longer existed. The breakup with the Bhopal family took a while to heal. I placed the experience in the category of, "Lessons learned while on the path of life."

Our small group of four headed south to the city of Puri. I felt the need to be near the ocean. Pavitra desired to find a school to learn how to weave cloth. Jack and Annie came with us for a few days but they wanted to return to Ceylon. Both of them visited the island country several years before. Today the country is called Sri Lanka. They said goodbye. We promised to keep in touch.

Within a few days of being in Puri, Pavitra found a school for weavers. I returned to the ashram to retrieve the surfboard Don left two years before. The young swami remembered me. He told me he used the board to paddle out beyond the surf and watch the people on the beach and float in the water. I promised to return the board when we left Puri.

Pavitra and I bought the necessities to cook and eat at the small beach apartment we rented. The dwelling was located a block from the ocean and included a palm branch roof, sand floor in the courtyard and a small sleeping room next to the kitchen. A large orange cat was included in the rent. Every day the feline jumped the complex wall into our courtyard. He made sure we threw nothing into the trash. He ate everything. I do not think we needed to empty the garbage once during the time we spent in Puri.

Puri fishermen showing their boating skills

The author and surfboard in Puri, India 1975

In the mornings Pavitra went to the weaving class and I headed to the beach to see if any waves were breaking. Every time I went to the beach I attracted the many children living there. These young beachcombers belonged to the fishermen who caught the fish in the area. The children waited for the moment I finished surfing. I let them play with the board and paddle around in the surf when I completed the day of surfing.

These children never experienced anything like a surfboard. As well as never seeing a surfboard, the sight of a person standing on the floating object and riding the waves coming into the shore just about 'blew their minds.' I wish I gave them the surfboard when I left Puri. Had I left the surf stick with these children the little beach urchins would have become the first generation of surfers in India. I am not aware if surfing exists in the subcontinent today but I suspect the fishermen children would have mastered the sport in a short amount of time.

Puri children with the first surfboard in India.

While staying in Puri, Pavitra and I decided to take a day trip to an ancient ruin only a few hours away by bus. The visit to the remains meant we needed to wake up before sunrise, catch a ride into town where the bus left from, eat breakfast and leave by 6 a.m. We accomplished all the steps including breakfast. As we ate in the restaurant I noticed an activity unfolding outside the building where we sat.

Puri is a holy city where Indian pilgrims travel in order to feed the poor and bathe in the ocean waters. I believe the ritual of emerging into the sea represented a cleansing of sins and the feeding the poor translated into the release of worldly possessions. The Indians involved in the holy journey to Puri would walk down the main street leading to the ocean. The street happened to be right outside the building where Pavitra and I were eating our breakfast.

The poor in Puri begging for rice or money from the pilgrims

Before the Indian pilgrims arrived, the beggars and physically deformed population of Puri arrived and started to mark out their spots along the route leading to the ocean. Most of the poor were thin and weather beaten from the sun. They represented the poverty population of India. As I continued to watch the activity through the window of the restaurant I noticed a normal young man, about twenty-five years of age, spread a small mat on the ground across the street from where we ate our meal. He carried in his arms a large number of bed sheet strips, stained and filthy from use. The young man proceeded to sit on the mat and began to wrap his body with the strips of sheets starting with his feet and continuing all the way up his torso including his head. By the time he finished he could have auditioned for the Indian version of "The Return of the Mummy," and easily been awarded the part.

A few minutes after the transformation of the young man into a bandaged beggar a bus, packed with pilgrims, arrived and they began the walk to the sea in order to cleanse their sins. Most of the wealthy Indians carried a sack of rice and a sack of picas or small change. As they proceeded down the path towards their salvation they placed rice and coins into the bowls of the many beggars along the route. No one suspected the mummy man as an imposter and he also received his share from the pilgrims making the walk towards the ocean.

After eating our meal I walked out into the street in order to take a photograph of the line of impoverished population accepting the gifts of the wealthy. Several Indians seemed a little agitated with my wanting to record the event so I stopped after one or two images. I did not take a photo of the man wrapped up like a mummy because our bus started to board. We had to leave in order to go to the ruins a few hours drive from Puri.

I assume such a story might lead the reader into making a judgment about this individual. "How could a healthy man do such a thing?" "He should get a job in order to support himself." Not knowing the man's situation we rush towards a verdict. I know I did. He might be supporting a family of five children or he could be getting rice so his sick parents can eat one meal a day.

We do not know the circumstances around the man's choice to do what he did but we still make our conclusions based on the limited insights of our own lives.

All religions have meaningful words of wisdom. The Christian Bible has a famous quote, "Judge not, least ye be not judged." The challenge many of us humans face is to use these spiritual insights in our lives.

*****

Puri is a holy city with a large temple in the middle of town. Entrance into the house of worship remained for Hindus only. One day, while shopping in a store outside the temple, I walked past the entrance and found a man stretched out on the pathway outside the temple door. He came to Puri to end his life. His body remained positioned near the front entrance. The torso wore nothing but a loincloth and a piece of material protecting him from the ground. Bones, covered by a thin layer of skin, made up the remains of the man. Indians do not get offended by death as we do in the States. Those Indians passing by the body realized he came to die at the temple. They did not interfere by rushing him off to a hospital or feeding him through a tube.

The next day I again came into town and walked near the temple. I wanted to see how the dying process played out in the Indian culture. Someone covered the body with a white cotton cloth since my last visit. The man remained alive but death seemed imminent. People walking by tossed coins on the cloth to help pay for the wood needed to cremate the body after death. By the third day, when I returned again to the location of the dying man, the body no longer remained outside the gate walls. The man died and I heard from a storekeeper the remains were taken into the Hindu temple to be cremated.

Death is accepted by Indian society. Everyone helps in the transition. I remained deeply moved by the three-day experience. I now possess a respect for Indians and the way they care for their own people. In the case of the dying man, no one knew him. Still, those who were able helped pay for the transition of the body in a caring manner. The strong belief in reincarnation probably allows the Hindu population to accept death much more than those religions in the West.

Chapter 48
Bodh Gaya and Varanasi

After a month of weaving lessons and surfing with the beach children of Puri Pavitra and I decided to move on. We decided to visit two holy sites in India. Bodh Gaya is where Gautama Buddha reached enlightenment beneath the Bodhi tree. Varanasi is where Hindus bathe in the Ganges to free themselves from sins. On the banks of the river, the dead are cremated and their ashes are dumped into the river. Most Hindus want their ashes put into the Ganges after death. With a population of over a billion people, the Burning Ghats can be quite busy.

In Bodh Gaya, we did one last meditation course for ten days. During the course I experienced another interesting event while sitting. My meditations seemed to become deeper and more concentrated. The fifth day, while doing the sweeping practice of Vipassana, I felt an energy surge starting at the base of my spine. The force went right up my back and out the top of my head. My consciousness and quiet observing mind followed the sensation and I seemed to be somewhere above my body looking down. I know I remained in this state of concentration for a period of time but I did not know how many minutes passed. All of a sudden a thought came to me.

"How do I get back to my body?"

Along with the thought, the feeling of fear also arose. My heart started beating quickly and in the next moment I returned to my body. I opened my eyes and looked around the room. Everyone in the meditation class sat in the same place as when the hour-long meditation began. Nothing seemed out of the ordinary. I sat and waited for

the end of the sitting in a dazed state. I remembered
Goenka's words.

"Do not become attached to any sensations or
experiences while meditating. Only observe them. Do
not run away from or grasp onto anything during
meditation."

During meditation, the balanced mind does not label
anything manifesting as good or bad. The balanced mind
only observes without attachment or avoidance.

The event happened just as I described; an experience
and nothing more. I do not try to repeat the energy rush
through my body nor do I avoid having the occurrence
happen again. It just was and I let it go.

One other situation happened at the course. I need to
bring up the story for the reader to protect them from a
similar discomfort. If you ever go to India and
participate in some type of meditation, be mindful of who
you wait behind in line. Some westerners take the vows
of Buddhism and become monks or nuns. They may
attend a course where you are practicing.

There were several such monks attending the last
course I took in Bodh Gaya. Everywhere they went each
step was made in slow motion. The practice used by the
monks as they walked from room to room is called
walking meditation. The object is to become aware of
each step one takes while traveling by foot. The slow
motion can take the monks ten times as long to move
from one place to another compared to a normal pace or
stride.

One afternoon I found myself in dire need of a
bathroom break. In India and most places in the east
such urgent bodily releases can arise quickly and with
little warning. This particular distress did not compare to

the Afghan bus ride adventure of several years before. Bathrooms were limited in the building where the retreat was held. The bathroom designer used a construction method adding time to the whole experience. The user of the WC would enter the room, shut the door behind them and walk about twenty feet to the toilet.

By the time I reached the line in front of the men's W.C. I knew I did not have much time before pain set in. Can the reader guess who stood in front of me also waiting for use of the bathroom? The orange colored robe is not what I wanted to be stuck behind. Every step he took, as the men before us finished their ritual, took place like a mime practicing a running sequence and traveling nowhere.

Finally, the monk took his turn. He entered the bathroom, slowly closed the door and set off towards the toilet itself. If a normal person walking with a standard speed of time needed two minutes to use the facility and walk back to the entrance I knew I needed to add more time for the monk. As the discomfort increased my mind imagined the monk in slow motion making his contemplative walk across the floor to the throne. Every step he took remained in total awareness. I could have practiced pain control meditation because discomfort is what I felt the whole 15 minutes he needed for his bathroom break. I was not generating good thoughts by the time the door re-opened. I covered the distance to the porcelain seat of relief in record time.

Remember readers, become aware of monks in orange robes practicing walking meditation when duty calls. Bathroom needs can be sudden and powerful while traveling in the east.

Before the course ended I was able to get a personal meeting with Goenka. He allowed students to visit him in the afternoon to discuss personal matters and seek his wisdom. I was still troubled with how the situation turned out with Mahendra and the money that I gave him. I felt cheated and hurt and could not stop the thoughts of anger arising towards my ex-friend. After telling Goenka the whole story, he looked at me and asked,

"Are you in need of money right now? Are you safe and in need of anything at all?"

"No" I answered.

"Then this is where you need to be," was his reply.

Just as he said the last statement I felt a wave of energy flow through me and all thought of remorse regarding the Mahendra discussion were gone and I was alone with Goenka. Somehow he cleared my thoughts and brought me to the core of Buddhism and other spiritual teachings. He brought me to the moment of "Now". In the "Now" there are no thoughts of past or future. You are simply where you are and there is not room for anything other than "Being Here Now". From that moment on I knew I was always safe when I was in the moment and the process of healing the Mahendra situation had begun.

Pavitra and I said our goodbyes to Goenka when the ten-day course finished. We left for Varanasi the next day. I would not see our teacher until 1983 when he came to California to teach a course in Mendocino. I still hold a place in my heart for this man and all other teachers of meditation in the world. They give of themselves knowing they are helping humans to become peaceful in their lives and more loving.

"May all beings be happy."

Upon arriving in Varanasi we first went to the bathing Ghats. At the Ghats, I hired a barber to shave my head. I walked down the stairs to submerge myself in the brown waters of the Ganges River. If I wanted to rid myself of sin I needed to trust I would not catch any disease by going into the river. I emerged, rinsed off and made my way back to the dressing chambers. Nothing in my health status changed over the next week so I assumed I washed away my sins, at least for the moment.

Bathing Ghats in Varanasi on the Ganges River.

Stories heard while traveling are the best. Many of them, after personal editing, have become legend and cannot be proven or disproven. I wondered why so many Indians who bathe in the Ganges River, including myself, do not become ill or contact a disease of some kind. Ashes of the many corpses burned each day are deposited in the river. Unburned bodies of holy men who die are also placed into the river. Sadhus and other gurus usually are not cremated and I never received an answer to the reason for the practice. I did see bodies in the Ganges so I assumed they were holy men.

The story of why no one gets sick from bathing in the river is due to a radioactive deposit of ore up stream from Varanasi. The radiation from the deposit kills any diseases or possible contaminants in the water. The reason I did not get sick from the dirty waters of this holiest of rivers, according to the tale or legend, is due to the germs receiving a radiation zap. I do remember maintaining a glow after my submersion into the waters for several days.

*****

The last town visited by Pavitra and me before leaving India had a name known around the world. Darjeeling, a hill station town built by the English, is famous for its' tea fields and cool summer temperatures. Pavitra desired to visit Darjeeling because her grandfather started a church in the town and lived there for a number of years. She never met her grandfather because he passed away long before she was born.

The best part of the journey to Darjeeling is the train ride up the mountain. To make this journey even possible the English built a smaller train and narrower gauged tracks to accommodate the difficult terrain. The ride consisted of passenger cars with locomotives on both ends of the train. As one engine pulled the other engine pushed.

The tracks lay out like a twisted snake. They included many switchbacks and bends built into the mountain. The engineers also used gravity to help get the travelers to their destination. When the train came to a steep part of the hill a section of track as long as the whole section of cars and locomotives was located past the curve in the tracks. The train would roll onto this long section and stop.

A view of the train tracks as they wind up the valley into Darjeeling.

The tracks would be switched over for the train to head up the next section of the hill. The rear engine would now be the puller and the previous front engine would now be the pusher. The linked cars used gravity to move downward towards the bend in the track and then uphill at the point where the tracks switched over to the new section.

The train trip up the hill included young children running along beside the passenger cars hopping on when they got tired and off when they needed to move to another car. They sold everything from tea to homemade meals their mothers cooked. Food is always available when you travel on a train in India. Fried vegetables and other items made every morning completed the menu for the ride up the hill.

Darjeeling maintained the look of a small English village. The architecture of the churches and buildings resembled those of Great Britain. Homes built by the wealthy families in India surrounded the town. Many housed, at one time, the highest ranked leaders of government during the 170 years of British rule.

Pavitra located the church her grandfather founded. As I stood in front of the Church of England I tried to imagine Darjeeling 100 years before. The streets would be filled with English women protected from the sun by their parasols. The ladies, accompanied by their servants, strolled through avenues and shopping districts buying the needed items for their household. At four in the afternoon, the shoppers would stop for the English ritual, tea. Teahouses could be found in abundance in this hill station providing the best drink in the English world.

While in Darjeeling we also met Tenzing Norgay, the Sherpa guide who climbed Mt. Everest with Sir Edmund Hillary. His job at the time we were in town included his presence at the Darjeeling Tourist-Center greeting tourists and posing for photographs with them. I knew who he was right away and I even took a picture of him with Pavitra. For me meeting Mr. Norgay remained an honor. He, still today, is the most famous climber and Sherpa guide in all of India and Nepal.

Tenzing Norgay with Pavitra in Darjeeling 1975

Chapter 49
Burma and South East Asia

Pavitra and I did not stay more than four days in Darjeeling. We needed to leave India and start our journey through South East Asia. Australia remained our destination and the distance seemed great when I looked at a map. I almost made the trip with Emil, my trekking buddy, several years before but I was stopped by the India-Pakistan war of 1971-1972.

We headed down the mountain and back to Calcutta where we obtained visas for Burma. Burma or Myanmar is the present name and it remained strict about the laws regarding the length of visas. The military government only allowed three days for tourists to come to their country. Three days allowed just enough time for tourists to land in Rangoon, take the long train ride north to Mandalay, view the temples and Buddhist monasteries, and then return to Rangoon. We decided not to spend our visa time on a long train ride. Instead, we landed in Rangoon and checked into a hotel in the city.

In 1975 tourists entering Burma could bring in two cartons of cigarettes obtained in the tax-free centers of the airports from which they departed. The cigarettes were valuable on the black market in Burma and the many taxi drivers waiting for people getting off the planes were ready to complete the transaction sale. Ten dollars represented the price for a carton in 1975. This brought the seller an eight-dollar profit from the tax-free cost. Sixteen dollars in Burma bought a night in a hotel. The cabbies then sold the western brand cigarettes to wealthy businessmen in Burma willing to pay $15 for the cigarettes. A profit of five-dollars brought a good supplement to a days pay for a Burmese taxi driver in 1975.

Besides visiting the main temple in Rangoon, Pavitra and I remained in the capital to visit the home and meditation center of U Ba Kim, Goenka's meditation teacher when he lived in Burma. Kim had long since passed on but others living at the center carried on Kim's work and teachings.

We arrived at the center in the afternoon. We presented ourselves and said we practiced meditation with Goenka while in India. Both of us received a nice welcome. For the next two days, Pavitra and I came out to the center to sit and meditate in the individual meditation cells. The cells surrounded a central room where the teacher would sit when a retreat took place. The meditation rooms appeared to be arranged in a circle much like a wheel with the spokes protruding out towards the individual cells. The number of cells seemed to be around twenty.

When we arrived in the afternoon we shared a meal with the family who ran the center, talked about our home countries and watched our breath for an hour in the center. Jack Fruit, a staple food at meals, was first given to me at lunchtime. Many foods, never seen or eaten before by us, appeared for the first time while in Burma. We even got to stay over for one night at the center. This happened due to the rains on our second evening. The tropical torrent came down so hard that getting to the bus for the ride back to town would have put us in jeopardy. The streets in Burma tend to flash flood during heavy rains. In tropical countries, the weather can dictate where you go and when.

On the third day, we took a taxi to the airport. Our time in Burma was over. At the airport, we saw many of the tourists who flew in with us and who took the train ride up to Mandalay. They appeared exhausted but said the city was beautiful and worth the trip.

I believe now the visas are longer when one visits Burma. I have heard they are now five days but the length of stay is subject to change depending on how the military rulers feel at the time. Burma (Myanmar) remains a military controlled country with little information coming out describing what goes on or how the government keeps people in line. The government, like all other repressive institutions in the world, struggles to keep their internal affairs private. The will of the people wanting to have more freedoms may win out some day and I hope the transition of power can be completed without bloodshed.

Young Buddhist Monks in Rangoon with gold leaf covering temples in background

Bangkok, the capital of Thailand, appeared in stark contrast to Rangoon. Vietnam fell to the communist army of North Vietnam just before we arrived in Thailand. Large numbers of American soldiers still remained in Bangkok either stationed there or on R&R. Many U.S. dollars were being spent on food, hotels, drugs and prostitutes. The economy in Thailand thrived while an American presence existed.

We stayed in one hotel full of GI soldiers and their companions. Pavitra and I took many of the tours around the city either by boat or bus. Buddhist temples filled the city and many of the more interesting ones could only be visited by boat. The hustle and bustle of city life in

Bangkok felt much more intense compared to the quieter and slower pace in Rangoon.

Our short stay in Bangkok was due to the fact we needed to get further south and on to Australia. We caught a bus out of the city and onto the main road heading south. We tried hitchhiking and eventually got a ride with a huge lumber truck.

The timber industry in 1975 remained a big business in the rainforest areas of Thailand. The hard teak wood and other exotic tree woods brought good prices from builders and wood carvers. The truck took us to a logger mill deep in the forest where we were able to catch one more ride to the next town before nightfall.

Finding a hotel in this town became an experience worth telling. Getting a room did not become a problem. We were a novelty to the owners and others who seemed to be staying there. The others included many young girls who seemed to be sitting around and waiting for something. It soon dawned upon us the girls were there for the lumbermen who worked all day cutting trees and harvesting the rain forest.

The lumbermen needed recreation and entertainment in the evenings. The girls filled the needs of the hard-working crews of men getting off work. The thin walls and late hours of the other inhabitants of the hotel left us with only a few minutes of deep sleep. The next morning we decided to catch a bus taking us directly to the border. We did not need to visit the many other logging camps and special hotels dotting the interior of Thailand.

Chapter 50
Ali, Ali

At the border of Thailand and Malaysia, a situation arose which is another story worth repeating. The date, June 30, 1975, became an important time in sports. Pavitra and I left the Thailand section of the border and entered the Malaysian border immigration office. Upon entering the building I noticed many young westerners sitting around as though they were waiting for something to happen. Whatever they waited for was taking a long time to happen. I talked to one of the American travelers and he said the border guards made all bearded men and travelers with long hair sit along the wall. No visas were being granted. Malaysia did not like hippies coming into their country. The guards hoped these western weirdoes would change their minds about traveling in Malaysia. In this part of the world guards and police have the power over one's ability to move.

I walked over to the immigration desk and noticed about four or five young men in uniform sitting around and talking with each other. They did nothing in the way of moving along the increasing numbers of western travelers sitting along the wall. The young guardians of Malaysia were listening to the radio and it sounded like a sports event.

All of a sudden I remembered from reading a paper in Bangkok this date, June 30, 1975, was the day Muhammad Ali fought Joe Bugner in Kuala Lumpur, Malaysia. For all you non-sports fans or people just too young to remember, the fight with Bugner preceded the "Thrilla in Manila" by three months. If you do not know what the "Thrilla in Manila" is then Google it. The excitement regarding the fight happening at the moment pertained to the fact it took place in the country Pavitra and I attempted to enter. I asked one of the border guards,

"Who is winning the fight?"

He looked at me in an inquisitive way. His expression told me he did not understand everything I said. I pointed to the little radio all the guards were listening to and stepped back from the counter. I raised my arms in a boxing position as though I wanted to take them all on and said again,

"Who is winning the fight?"

One of the guards who spoke the most broken English answered,

"Why? Who you like?"

He recognized my movements and question referred to the boxing match he and the other guards were listening to. My answer in the next moment would determine how fast I crossed into the country of Malaysia.

"Muhammad Ali" I answered.

"You like Muhammad Ali?" he shot back at me.

"Of course I like Muhammad Ali," I answered. "He's the best."

I limited my use of adjectives to describe the best fighter of all time because too many words get lost in translation. The short statement I gave seemed to be the correct answer to the "Sixty-Four Thousand Dollar Question." This is another reference to trivia anyone fifty years old or younger might not have knowledge about. Google it.

The guard said something to the other border guards in their native tongue. All at once they all jumped up and down like they just won the Malaysian lottery. The connection between the guards and the fight is as follows. Malaysia is a Muslim country and Muhammad Ali converted to Islam years before. Ali became a Muslim while fighting the American government. The U.S. tried to draft Muhammad into the military and send him to Vietnam, a war Ali stood against and publicly voiced his opposition. After stripping Ali of his title and his ability to fight in the States several boxing matches were set up in different foreign countries. All the best fighters wanted to take on Ali. The fights took place in foreign Muslim countries and became big news as well as big money makers.

The match today took place in Malaysia and everyone here wanted Muhammad Ali to win. All the guards came over to the counter and started practicing their own broken English on me in an attempt to show their joy in the fact I liked Muhammad Ali. To them, Ali remained a sports hero for their country and religion. One of the guards said,

"Give me passport."

He took Pavitra's and my passport, stamped them and said,

"You go now."

He pointed to the train waiting to take us to the next town in Malaysia.

As this incident unfolded all the other travelers waiting along the walls of the building for hours in order to get a stamp in their passport looked at Pavitra and me as we exited the building. Their mouths hung open in shock. I could not tell if any of them overheard the exchange with the guards or if the name Muhammad Ali meant anything to them. This is one time it paid to be a sports fan and root for the "right" winning player.

Chapter 51
Thirty-Five Years Later

On the weekend of February 14, 2009, my wife, Suzanne, and two other friends, Scott and Pam, went to a Phoenix nightclub we heard about. We went there to listen to some jazz. A small dance area in front of the club stage allowed about four couples to dance to the music. The singer and her band stood right behind the dance floor. After a music set, we were able to squeeze onto the floor and strut our stuff. Yes at 63 I still strut.

As the dancing began I noticed the table right next to the area where we stood. The top of the table contained pieces of paper and drawings all over them. The large man sitting at the table with six other friends seemed busy working on another piece of art. He faced to his right and sat hunched over his work. I could not see his face. I saw the woman next to him and I recognized her at once from the many news clips while accompanying her husband. Mrs. Ali sat next to the man working on art drawings. I again looked at the man next to her and he now faced the dance floor. It was the greatest fighter of all time sitting at the table listening to jazz and making art pictures.

I turned to Scott and said,

"Scott, I think Muhammad Ali is sitting at the table with his wife."

Scott confirmed my observation and agreed with me that the man sitting in the chair six inches from me was Ali. I needed to say something to the couple. I still carried the story of the border crossing into Malaysia in my head and I repeated the story over and over again for the last 35 years. My moment to thank Ali for being there for me finally arrived. Ali, though he never met me, needed to hear the story.

Returning to our table I went up to Mrs. Ali and asked,

"Can I tell you a story?"

She remained gracious and said yes. I began to tell her the story of the border crossing into Malaysia and how her husband helped me get into Malaysia 35 years before. She told me when she and Ali travel to those Muslim countries they are still treated like heroes and are given the utmost respect. I thanked her and she in return thanked me for the story. I hope she repeated it to her husband at some other time. I felt privileged to have caught sight of Ali, meet his wife and retold the tale of "The Great Crossing."

Malaysian boys having fun on the beach

Chapter 52
Malaysia, Indonesia, and Bali

On our trip through Thailand, we heard of a pleasant village beach town on the west coast of Malaysia. Many beautiful beach towns exist in Malaysia but I did not write the name of the one we visited so I cannot recommend it to the reader. We stayed on the beach for about a week eating good rice and Malaysian dishes while resting up after our long road trip through Thailand.

Malaysia has a military government. The presence of the army throughout the nation did not seem to affect the people. They were just as warm and friendly as the population in Thailand. The citizens of these junta political parties are not affected by whoever rules. They all have jobs to do in order to make money and work does not seem to involve the politics surrounding them.

Pavitra and I decided to catch a train all the way through Malaysia to Singapore. A communist insurgent presence throughout the country existed in 1975 and hitchhiking would not be a good idea. We boarded the train going down the east coast of the country.

Military men patrolled the trains and made sure no weapons or other items considered dangerous or illegal existed in the luggage of passengers. The trains in Malaysia appeared to be newer compared to the Indian trains. Also, the cars were not overcrowded. Overpopulation in India compared to South East Asia makes a difference when traveling.

Upon our arrival at the border to Singapore, we found out luck continued to travel with us. The train going down the west coast came under attack by communist guerillas. Trouble caused by the army fighting off the insurgents and making repairs to the track made the west coast train a day late.

The border crossing into Singapore held no similarities to the previous border crossing. Malaysia, a third world country, and Singapore, a modern city on the same scale as any city in Europe or the United States, took me by surprise. The vast difference between these two countries separated by just a few miles, compared to driving from Tijuana, Mexico to San Diego. Most of the workers doing the menial labor jobs come over from Malaysia to earn the higher salaries. Skyscrapers completed the skyline in this modern city. Much of the trading wealth in the East, either in banking or business, passes through Singapore. The city remained clean and sterile. Anyone caught painting graffiti on walls receives a beating with a bamboo cane and are either extradited back to their country of origin or jailed if Singapore is their home.

We found a clean hotel at a good price and checked in. We decided to walk to the downtown restaurants. The eateries remained outside and under shade coverings to protect the clients from the intense Asian sun. Many different dishes of food could be found throughout the closely grouped places to eat. The food courts in the malls throughout the U.S. must have borrowed the idea of grouping restaurants together. Singapore did it in 1975, long before our malls came up with a similar idea.

Pavitra found it difficult discovering something to eat. She did not do well with all the food smells filling the air of these outdoor food courts. She decided to go to a doctor the next day and find out if she picked up a bug. I spent the next day trying to find out about traveling to the island of Sumatra in Indonesia. We both wanted to visit the island culture before we left for Australia.

The next afternoon I returned to the hotel and found Pavitra sitting on the bed, cross-legged and playing solitaire. She appeared nervous. All she said to me as she looked up in my direction was,

"I'm pregnant."

I remember the moment as if it were yesterday and not thirty-five years ago. Periods in the continuum of life stand out more than others. This was one such wrinkle in time. Men see their lives flash before their eyes. At this instant men either cut bait or fish. They become men or remain little boys and look for an escape from the unknown.

At the age of thirty, my life of traveling throughout Europe, Africa, Asia and South East Asia appeared to be ending. Could I stop traveling the world and start focusing my life on something more stable in order to make room for another person to come into it? I sat down. In this moment I knew life, as I knew it, was about to change. I decided to fish.

Pavitra relaxed upon seeing my positive reaction to the prospects of having a child. She did not know what I would do. I sat down and we knew we needed to make some travel changes. Skipping a trip to Sumatra became the first item on our list. The conditions are more primitive there and being pregnant does not translate into roughing it. Getting closer to Australia in the near future became our focus. We prepared to travel through Indonesia a little faster knowing a baby would soon make an appearance and change our lives forever.

Indonesian Dancer

We sailed from Singapore to Jakarta on the island of Java. We landed in the country of Indonesia were Jakarta is the capital. This part of the travel became a little blurred in my memory. Thinking about a baby coming into our lives affected my travel recall ability. I do remember going to some of the tourist shows which include shadow puppet dancers, the Monkey Dance done by male dancers and the good food of Indonesia.

Travel through the island of Java was easily accomplished by bus. From the southern end of the island, we took a boat to Bali, an island paradise, where we stayed for a month. We rented a room in a beach hotel on the shores near the town of Kuta. Bali is an island where Australian vacationers travel to unwind and experience the culture of their northern neighbor. Many surfers from the 'land down under' also make Bali a destination during the high surf months. During August and September, the waves broke big and the surfer numbers were high.

Bali Medicine Man

The stay in Bali became a regrouping time for Pavitra and myself. The doctor in Singapore gave us an idea when the baby was conceived and we now knew which month the baby would be born. January seemed like a good time to come into the world especially if one lives south of the equator. Summer and warm weather exist and life around the Barbie, Australian slang for barbecue, remains the lifestyle in Aussie Land.

August in Bali meant only six months separated us from the need to be in a place of stability. Being a future parent of a child coming into the world, one tends to make long-range plans. I started to feel roots growing out of my feet. I needed to get somewhere and plant them. This period in life became a major transition time for both Pavitra and myself.

Bali, as I mentioned before, sported big waves and many tourists. August is the end of winter. The storms hitting the beaches made ten and twelve foot swells and attracted some of the best surfers in the world. Most of them came from Australia where surfing and wave riding is a national sport.

By now surfing and I experienced a six years divorce not counting the moments I tried it in Puri, India and with Don as we traveled the shores of India. Seeing the Australian men ripping the Bali waves really inspired me to get out there again. A couple of Bali boys owned a nine-foot board and were generous enough to let me borrow it. I usually found them on the beach every day and I waited until they were finished with their efforts in the ocean. I stayed inside and caught the smaller waves around three or four feet in size. I managed a few rides and re-stoked the fire I possessed for the sport. Surfing used to be called the Sport of Kings in Hawaii because only royalty were allowed to surf. Only a surfer would really know what I am talking about. It gets into your blood and never goes away. I am 65 and I still watch surfing movies and events on TV.

Surfing is not like riding a bicycle. One needs to practice the sport constantly in order to keep in shape and master the timing. Being away from wave riding for a few years and trying to return to the skill level one used to have is a slow process. Bali became the last place I ever surfed. Not a bad place to remember when you vision the last wave you caught. Surfing became one more thing I let go as I headed into parenthood.

While on Bali, Pavitra and I visited a famous artist. I do not recall his name but Indonesia is known for having some of the best carvers in the world. The fame of this man attracted wealthy politicians and world leaders who placed orders with him. Some of these orders would take years to complete. He even carved epic Hindu stories onto elephant tusks. Such a work remained on display in the store set up to sell carvings the artist completed. The oldest son took us around the workshop and gift store while the father entertained guests while he worked on a project at the same time. In 1975 the restrictions on African and Indian ivory did not exist or were not enforced as they are today.

Full Moon Wedding in Bali

One of the big events we planned, while on the island of Bali, was a wedding on the beach during the August full moon of 1975. We met several people from the states who wanted to participate in this event. We even found a young man who was a minister through The Universal Life Church. The Universal Life Church gave minister licenses to anyone who applied. Many men who objected to the Vietnam war became ministers in an attempt to dodge the draft. This man happened to be in Bali on vacation from the Peace Corps. He joined the Corps as an alternative to going to Vietnam.

While on Bali a military coup in Bangladesh took place and our future minister could not get back into the country until the new government reopened its' borders. What a place to be stranded while waiting for the borders to reestablish passage. Palm trees, white sandy beaches, and delicious Indonesian food made for a pretty nice place of exile.

Two friends, Robert and Kate, were on Bali at the time. We met them in India at a meditation retreat and we reconnected with them on the island. They put a lot of effort into the wedding and became our wedding party. A Buddhist who lived on the island also came to the wedding. We eventually counted twenty-five people at the ceremony enjoying any reason for a party.

Buddhism used to have a strong foothold in Indonesia. Bali today remains a Hindu island because of the difficult seas surrounding its' shores protecting the population from the forceful spread of the religion of Islam. Many of the Hindu population of Indonesia found safety in the 16th century from the Islamic spread throughout the region. Ninety-four percent of the people on the island practice their version of Hinduism, which came from India many years before.

On the night of the full moon, flowers and magic mushrooms arrived on the beach. Pavitra and I dressed up in Bali wedding clothing complete with crowns and silk sarongs. We wrote out a marriage certificate, stamped the parchment with Balinese stamps and asked the local postman in the beach post office to sign across the stamps in order to make the manuscript official.

A few weeks later when we attempted to enter Australia as a married couple the immigration people got a good laugh when we showed them the marriage certificate. We were told to re-marry when we got to Sydney. The wedding paper may be official in Bali but Australian officials did not place any value on the parcel and to them, we were not married.

Wedding Party in Bali

Chapter 53
Australia 1975

With the wedding ceremony complete we prepared to head further south to Australia with a quick stop on the island of Timor. This is the last in the chain of islands stretching all the way from Singapore to Australia. Several of the islands still contained populations of people who do not have much contact with the outside world.

The flight to Timor from Bali passed over several islands thickly covered in tropical vegetation. As we departed from the small island hopper plane in Timor I noticed a man dressed in shorts with a backpack over his shoulder standing near the plane. He stood without moving and kept his gaze on the large bird from the sky. The metal winged animal just landed and people exited from a door in the belly. This may have been the first time the Timor islander ever saw a plane up close. A local islander working at the small airport told me the man probably came from a small village in the interior of the island. He just arrived by foot to see the new world for the first time. I can only imagine the thoughts going through the native's head as he came into contact with the 20th century.

Even today tribes of villagers may be living in remote areas of the world, isolated from outside populations. Planes may fly over their houses but none have experienced what these flying birds look like on the earth. The moment of the first contact would be overwhelming for any of them. They may just stare like the native did with our plane. Timor, in 1975, remained a location where the past met the present.

Darwin, located at the top of Australia, became our first town we visited. After the plane landed and before we could exit, two immigration officers, dressed in shorts and knee socks, boarded the plane and began spraying the interior with some sort of mist. The spray was meant to kill any bugs or mites hitching a ride with any passenger on board. I do not know the effect of the gas on our lungs. We all breathed in the fumes as we departed the plane. I was, however, able to understand the Australian accent much better after inhaling the spray.

The city of Darwin appeared to be going through rebuilding in 1975. A hurricane struck the city earlier in the year and carpenters could be found everywhere rebuilding homes and businesses destroyed by

the high winds. Even the hotel in which we stayed received some damage and the pounding of hammers became our alarm clock early the next morning when we awoke. The short stay in Darwin did not allow us to see any sights in the area. Our need to head further south and get settled somewhere before January became the motivation moving us along.

Greg Berry, the person Pavitra traveled with into the region of Assam, India a few years before, met us in Brisbane. He returned to his homeland the year before. We boarded his small car and drove to Lismore, Australia where he lived at the time. In Lismore, we met several other people who visited India the same time as us. One person, in particular, was a young man named Charlie Owen.

Charlie, an Englishman, attended a meditation course with me in India and he happened to be visiting friends in Lismore. He said he lived in Bondi Beach in Sydney and we could stay with him until we could find a job and a place to live. I could not believe how fortunate it was to come across Charlie in the countryside of Australia. Our guardian angel continued looking after us even down here in the Land of Oz. Isn't life great when it gives you just what you need?

From Lismore we boarded the train to take us south. The train system in Australia is excellent and we arrived in Sydney after hours of travel. We made our way across town to Bondi Beach and the apartment of Charlie. He was happy to see us and made room in his small apartment for our sleeping and living. I think Charlie wanted company and our visit to his home fit the bill.

Charlie lived about two blocks away from one of the most beautiful and famous beaches in the city of Sydney, Bondi Beach. Early mornings kayakers appeared in the bay, paddling across the waters. When the waves picked up surfers appeared and did their thing. The community, much like many of the beach towns lining the southern coast of California, expressed the relaxed lifestyle one finds while living near the water. The main difference separating coastal California and coastal Australia is the shark nets. They are needed to protect bathers from becoming a meal for the population of man-eaters patrolling the waters just outside the protected areas of cove beaches and waterway. Without the nets, the sparse population of Australia would remain small and no one could enjoy the many water sports this country provided.

On a walk around the beach town of Bondi, I came across a surfboard shop selling Gordon & Smith surfboards. This information would only be of interest to a surfer who grew up in Pacific Beach, San Diego. On Grand Ave. near where my father practiced dentistry, Larry Gordon and Floyd Smith opened their first surfboard shop. I spent many Saturdays in their shop when I was a teenager in San Diego. I was amazed to find they expanded all the way to Australia.

We stayed for about a month with Charlie at Bondi Beach. During our stay in Sydney Pavitra and I got married at the city courthouse making the union official in the eyes of the government. I still have the wedding parchment with the stamps and signatures from Bali. Pavitra did not seem to enjoy the energy of city life so we began searching the country around Sydney for a place to live. We bought an Australian car called a Holden and found a house in a community called Agnus Banks near the town of Richmond. The town is located an hour's drive north of Sydney towards the Blue Mountains and contained many market garden farmers from Greece and other Mediterranean countries.

The owner of the house, a Greek market farmer named Lazzaris grew corn in the summer and cauliflowers in the winter. He sold his crops at the main vegetable market in Sydney. Lazzaris lived in the town of Richmond due to the fact he needed to live closer to a hospital. A heart attack the year before did not seem to slow him down much. Every day he worked his ten- acre field. We rented his old house right in the middle of the cauliflowers and corn.

While in Sydney I discovered outdoor and indoor markets throughout the city. A seller could rent a space and sell items to the public ranging from clothing to homemade knick-knacks. I acquired some beautiful blouses made in Bali along with some other items from Indonesia when traveling through months before. I soon built up a business selling clothing in three of the markets throughout the city. The demand for items made in the east such as India and Southeast Asia continued to provide Pavitra and me with an income.

Soon after starting the business and moving out to Agnus Banks, Rob and Kate, the couple from Bali who helped with our wedding, joined us in our house. They were completing a trip around the world and Australia remained the last country to visit before returning home. By the time they arrived the business and life started to flow.

Rob and I would go to the markets for three days during the week and Kate would stay with Pavitra who by now showed the effects of the pregnancy.

An interesting anomaly happened with Rob and me while working the markets. Every other week or so a group of young Australian girls started to hang around our clothing stall. They sometimes bought skirts or blouses and other times all they wanted to do was talk. One day I asked them why they liked hanging around our clothing stall and chatting with us. Their answer surprised me.

"We like hearing your way of speaking. We do not hear American accents much and we like hearing you two talk."

All this time I thought the Australians were the ones who spoke with an accent. I realized now we were the foreigners and our way of speaking meant we spoke with an accent. The things you learn while living in a foreign country.

Rob and Kate both came from the States. After a couple of months in Australia, the desire for them to return overcame the need to stay. Both returned in December to America.

Kate helped open a meditation center in Massachusetts and Rob started a business taking Americans to India to tour and practice meditation. Hello, Rob and Kate wherever you are now.

By the middle of December Ray and Deborah arrived at our house in Agnus Banks from New Zealand. We met them while in Manali, India. They were friends of Greg Berry. They tried to buy land and practice the back to the land life style many people were doing in the 70's. New Zealand no longer allowed Australians to move to their country without going through the paperwork and scrutiny other countries faced. The couple could not make the situation work.

Deborah gave birth to a daughter named Willow three months before. Deborah, a trained nurse, became a wealth of information for Pavitra in her late stages of carrying a child. Deborah coped well in emergency situations, which I think is the reason she became a nurse.

When we were living in Bondi Beach Pavitra made a connection with a midwife and wanted to use her to deliver the baby. Since we now lived in the country we needed to prepare in advance for the midwife. The house, located an hours drive from Sydney, presented a timing problem. We would need to have the midwife at our home for the birth.

Midwives seemed to be more plentiful in Australia than the U.S. in 1976. The reason for the need of midwives pertained to the large population of rural farmers and cattle ranchers filling the countryside. Getting to a hospital may not always be the easiest solution. Having a midwife come to the house for the birth worked much better for the rural lifestyle of this vast country in the 70s.

Christmas came and went. Turkey cooked on the Barbie, while dressed in shorts and a tee shirt, remained something I would never really get used to even though I would spend the next three and a half years in Australia. I also started to understand more about the Australian culture the longer Pavitra and I lived with Ray and Deborah.

The time for baby number one approached. I filled my week with work at the outdoor markets, bought clothing for the following week and improved the mobile stall used to hang and present the clothing. I even made a loom in my spare time and began to weave a Tibetan style carpet. I needed to stay busy with a project to help keep centered during my wait.

January 15, 1976, arrived and the signs of the expected birth presented themselves. Men learn a lot about giving birth when they are present for the whole process. Pavitra's water broke and the phone call to the midwife came next. It took several hours for the midwife to find our house. She arrived just in time for the event. No cell phones in 1976. Next time we decided we would go to her instead of her coming to us.

The contractions came close together. Before the midwife arrived, Deborah helped in every way possible to get Pavitra ready. Some birth trauma existed, according to the midwife, due to the cord being around the neck of the baby. She came out a little on the blue side close to the color of the deep tropical waters in Caribbean calendar pictures. Soon the baby regained her normal color when the air passage cleared. The midwife suggested we take the baby to the nearest hospital in Richmond to have her checked out. At age thirty I grew my first of many gray hairs during the experience.

The time must have been 4:00 am when we arrived at the hospital. The nurses were not happy about the fact we just completed a home delivery and started to warn us of the complications connected with a home birth. The midwife came with us to the hospital but she hung back not wanting to get into a confrontation with the hospital. She used to be a hospital nurse herself. She became a midwife after the hospital, where she had her baby five years before, made a mistake and the baby died.

Sukita, the name of our baby, received an examination and was cleared of any complications. Pavitra spent the day at the hospital and returned home the evening of January 16, the official birth date. Little did we know but exactly one and a half years from this date we would be doing this again in a different location with a different situation. Good thing I look good in gray.

The next year life seemed to settle into a routine. Ray and I worked the clothing business together with regular visits from friends at our country home. Our landlord, Lazzaris, used to visit us all the time but did not come around anymore. He would only drop in when Ray and Deborah vacated the house to visit family in Sydney.

I soon realized racism existed not only in America but also in Australia. Being from Greece the skin of Mediterranean populations such as Lazzaris tended to be dark. To some Australians like Ray the term 'Wog' replaced the N word in America. I learned not to get into conversations about this subject with Ray. Anyone of color and not a white Australian was considered a 'wog'. As in America, Australia also contained a population of ignorant whites who needed to look down upon someone or something in order to feel good about themselves.

Chapter 54
Mate

Another lesson learned about the Australian culture pertained to their history. Australia, unlike the United States, did not start as a religious refuge for people too radical for Europe. Australia began as a penal colony. The first immigrants were sent to the southern hemisphere to serve time for their crimes. Later when England wanted to expand Australia into becoming a large colony, women became the cargo of choice. A country needs a female population if they want to increase the number of people living there. The women became the wives of the free men and ex-convicts. Without them, the country would have simply died off.

Because the "fairer sex" came much later to Australia many years passed in which free white males hung out with each other. A term used in Australia, which I never heard before, was 'mate.' The term is a part of the male Australian culture today. If two blokes called themselves mate then they did everything together. They hunted, drank, went on trips and confided with each other. I do not know how well the movie "Broke Back Mountain" went over in Australia but from what I could see about couple relations of Australia in 1976, similarities remained.

I am not saying the relationship with mates is sexual. I am saying there seemed to be a carry over to Australia in 1976, based upon the historical relations of the men. In the 70s the bars were segregated. Men drank in one section and women and children were only allowed in another portion of the pub. Men justified this separation by saying they did not want women to be around men when they drank and swore. Australian men felt the two worlds, swearing, and drinking, went together.

I saw the separation of men and women as a carryover from Australia's historical roots. I did so from an observer's eye and not as a person who grew up accepting the tradition as a way of life. Things have changed a lot in Australia just as in America but in 1976 an American woman would not have put up with such male, female segregation and the custom called 'mate.'

Chapter 55
Back to the Land

While we started to settle into parenthood, the desire of Pavitra, Greg, Ray and Deborah along with another friend, Tim, from Britain, to buy land, build houses and get away from city life, continued. Back to the land movements existed in America in the 70's as well. All of us, babies included, traveled to several sites to check out properties for sale. One place called Taree was about a six-hour trip by car northeast of Sydney and became a place of interest. Taree was built on the coast like most Australian towns and became the main center from where we stayed as we viewed the land. Elands' is the name of the dairy and lumber community. It is located one and a half hours inland amongst the gum tree forest of New South Wales.

The name Elands comes from an antelope in Africa. I have no idea how the word made its' way to Australia. The asking price for the parcel was $4000. The size of property included 1,400 acres. A small creek ran through the real estate providing water all year round. A group decision came shortly after visiting the property. We made the purchase. Our lifestyle would change drastically for the next two and a half years.

The move to the country seemed easy for all the other land buyers in our group. None of them owned a business, which needed to be sold, or owned any furniture, which needed to be transported. Ray became frustrated with working at the markets. All he could think about he expressed in these words,

"I can hardly wait until we are moved to Elands. Everything will be fine once we are away from the city and living in the country."

The move away from the city became the answer, or at least he hoped, to all his problems. During the time Ray lived with us I noticed he possessed a few such internal demons. Drinking became a big part of covering up those tribulations. Alcohol also played a big part as the national pastime of Australia. I wonder what all the troubles being covered up by alcohol were?

Greg, Ray, and Deborah set out to Elands months before Pavitra and me. The idea of opening a clothing store in Taree held no support by the other land partners. Their idea of living on the dole (unemployment) and building homes in the country held little merit for me as a perfect lifestyle. My ability to always find ways of making money as I did in Holland and Greece really went against the
grain of those wanting the 'do nothing and get paid for doing nothing' lifestyle.

For the next few months, I ran the clothing business alone and helped Lazzaris harvest and sell his cabbages in the food market on Saturdays. Our landlord started to come around the house and visit again. Ray and Debbie no longer occupied the front room. I believe Lazzaris felt the negative vibrations Ray gave him when he dropped by so he did not visit during their time at the house.

After Ray and Debbie left for the country, I began to put the pieces together. Ray saw these hard working immigrants as stealers of jobs from white Australians. I believe the same comparisons are being made today in Arizona, Texas and a few other border states with Mexico. I see the hardest physical labor being completed in extreme heat and cold by a Spanish-speaking workforce. Some whites in the U.S. and Australia do not want to do hard, physical labor. In reality, all Ray wanted to do included drinking, smoking dope and collecting the dole. Can one conclude we might have a similar situation in this country?

After three months I sold the clothing business to some friends. Pavitra and I packed our car and bid farewell to Lazzaris and his family. We were now headed to the hillside community of Elands, Australia. We needed two days to make the drive.

When we arrived I could not believe the lack of accomplishments by the partners on the land. Building homes and moving from the small schoolhouse we rented did not see any progress whatsoever. The chickens Ray and Deborah brought with them were living on the front porch and shitting everywhere. Both our babies were crawling at the time and putting everything in their mouths. You can figure out the rest. Pavitra and I had moved into a home with a "do nothing" mentality. Getting paid for hanging out in the country seemed to be the main focus.

A few weeks passed and eventually the living arrangements came to a pressure head. The stress of having to do something constructive in order to move onto virgin real estate overwhelmed Ray. His wife spent much of her time justifying his inability to get motivated.

"We have not found a site to start building."

"Without a chainsaw and proper tools, we cannot do anything."

When Pavitra and I moved in and asked why there seemed to be no progress, Ray exploded. The country lifestyle did not mellow him. The reality of all the hard work needed to live off the grid and in the country became apparent. He could not sit around smoking dope and drinking beer. After the meltdown he moved to the property by himself.

With the help of Tim, Ray started to build a home. The design by the Englishman looked more like an erector set instead of a solid house with ninety-degree angles. It became the house never finished. To understand why such a dwelling was attempted one needs to understand the relationship between Tim and Ray.

Before attempting the Elands move Ray, Deborah, and Greg lived in a house somewhere in NSW. Tim also came to live with them. During their time together Ray became intrigued. When he talked about Tim during our time in the house outside Sydney he described him as one would describe a wizard such as Gandalf in the Lord of the Rings. Tim could do this or Tim knew about that. When I met the man for the first time I could see how easily one could become mesmerized by his personality and his attempts to come across as a wise sage.

Tim stood about 6' 4'' feet tall. His long graying hair went past his shoulders and the beard he sported grew straight down highlighting his long drawn face. Whenever he got into a conversation he would bring out a short, curly pipe and go through the routine of cleaning it, packing tobacco into the uniquely carve bowl, and lighting it over and over again. Tim never seemed to be relaxed when engaging in conversation. Instead, he appeared to be sizing the other person up and placing them in a category in which he could refer to when another speaking encounter took place.

Ray came from a different background. His education did not take him far. Surfing and a party lifestyle eventually landed him in jail for a short period. Home life for Ray lacked a father figure. His talents lay in the world of art. Some of the batik pieces he created hung on the walls of different relatives homes but the attempt to break into a gallery to market his ability never came to fruition. When Tim came into his life, Ray found the father figure he never knew. He seemed to hang on to every word spoken by this English wise man and in Ray's eyes Tim could do no wrong. Tim became a mentor for Ray and continued to guide him in a way only known to Tim.

A better picture of why such a hobbit style home was attempted in the first place should be in focus. Only the architect knew how the house of many curves could be accomplished and Ray did not. He went along with Tim's plans as best he could because he wanted so much to be like the man from Britain. Several years later, when the house still remained in an unfinished state, Tim received blame for why Ray could not complete the project. Are we starting to see a pattern here?

Soon after Ray left the schoolhouse, Pavitra and I made our move to live on the land. We first found a spot on a flat ridge across the Doyles River, which flowed through the property. We bought a small trailer and moved it onto the plot of land. Next to the trailer I built a tiny kitchen. We placed a wood-burning stove in the kitchen and hauled water up from the river every three days. A Land Rover with four-wheel drive became our main transportation and workhorse.

The next two years became the most physical period of my life. Moving back to the country and living off the grid from 1976 to 1979 molded my thinking process. While homesteading in Australia I learned I could accomplish anything if I put my mind to it. The secret to success, 'keep doing a little bit each day.'

November of 1976 became the next period of change for Pavitra and me. Our second child was due in July. I started building the main house and spent most of the daylight hours on construction. The home would be our residence for the duration of our stay in Australia.

Ray and Deborah moved back to Sydney. More money needed by them could be earned in the city. Vehicles and tools needed to be purchased in order to make the life in the country possible. Tim returned to Japan to be with his Japanese wife, Junko. She came to live with Tim on the land but after giving birth to a son she returned to Japan to visit her parents. Greg was the only other owner still living on the property and he filled his day building his house. We now lived on the property without distractions or drama.

The year became a constructive time for us. Not only did I complete the house I also built a house for our goats and fenced off the garden from the wild animals. We contracted a dam to be built above our site so we could gravity feed the garden and fruit trees planted. I never built anything before and here I am living the life of an Australian homesteader in the country.

Interior of home built by author.

During this constructive period we made closer friendships with others who accomplished the same thing we were attempting. One particular person whom I found most interesting originally came from America. His name was Gladney Oakley. He moved to Australia ten years before, married and became the father of two children. He divorced several years before we arrived in Australia. As a chemist in the 60's he made large sums of money making and selling LSD in Sydney during the Timothy Leary years. Yes, I guess the period of the 'Love Generation' even made it down to Australia. He now owned an apple farm complete with farm and orchard. He lived by himself like the sage on the hill overlooking a valley below. Blue became his trademark color. He must have purchased a shipment of JC Penny blue tee shirts and shorts in the past because those were the clothing items he wore all year long. In the winter a blue sweatshirt kept his upper body warm but his legs remained bare. During the two and a half years we lived in the town of Elands I saw Gladney wear long pants twice. Both times the weather reached extreme cold conditions.

His long hair and equally long beard were also trademarks of this American apple grower. Gladney became the local car mechanic teaching many of us how to replace car parts and get our vehicles ready for the yearly inspections we needed to complete so our cars and land rovers remained legal. Gladney also pursued a spiritual path. Pavitra became a spiritual friend and helped him with his meditation practice.

During the community gatherings held each month, Gladney brought a projector and showed films and cartoons for the adults and kids. He always had a number of children ages five and older hanging onto him and trying to wrestle the bearded sage to the ground. He became their favorite uncle and he loved all the children in the community.

Nardya and Andy were another couple, I respected in the community. They moved to Elands several years before, bought land and settled in. Andy, an engineer by trade, used his building skills to complete a beautiful home. The structure became an inspiration for myself and other homesteaders. Andy always became available when the time arose for helping others getting projects finished. I considered him one of the leaders of this developing community.

The industry in Elands primarily consisted of dairy farmers and lumbermen. A mill in town cut the smaller logs cut in the area. The bigger trees traveled by truck to the larger mill in Wingham forty miles away. In the center of town a tiny country store served as a post office and gas station. The population in 1977 numbered around 500 people.

School children traveled an hour on the bus to get to school in the town of Wingham only 30 miles from Elands. In winter the bus picked the children up in the dark and returned them again in darkness. There seemed to be little contact with the locals when we first moved to Elands. By the time we left in 1979 several of us started to go to the local community board meeting attempting to make our mark in the neighborhood.

Chapter 56
July 16, 1977

The evening of July 15, 1977 found us at home in Elands. We planned to drive to Sydney in a day or two to get settled at the home of our midwife and prepare for the birth of our second child. We remained two weeks from the expected due date. During the night around 10 p.m., Pavitra woke me and said,

"I think my water broke."

We remained unprepared for what followed.

"Alright, just go back to sleep and we will go to Sydney tomorrow," I answered.

"No, my water broke. We cannot wait until tomorrow. We have to do something now." Pavitra answered.

My obvious inexperience with water breaking and not knowing how much time remained before the baby came left me in the realm called,

'Oh crap, now what do I do?'

"I'll get the car ready. You get ready and I will get Sukita."

We lived an hour and a half drive from Taree where we knew there was a hospital. The car was low on gas and would not make the trip without more fuel. I held little cash because I needed no money unless I went shopping. We drove to the Elands store to fill up but all the lights remained off and no sign of life came from the house behind the store. Country folk go to bed early and do not want to be disturbed. We headed down the hill with the fuel needle hovering just above empty. I decided to coast as much as I could. We soon arrived at another small store at the bottom of the hill also serving as a gas station, post office and community center. A high school dance in the center next to the store entertained dozens of teens on this particular night.

"I need to get gas or we will not make it to Taree," I told Pavitra.

I got out of the car and continued knocking on the door of the store until the owner emerged. His facial expression told me he did not appreciate being disturbed from his sleep.

"My wife is having a baby and we are out of gas." I told him.

He immediately changed the expression on his face. He thought the knocking on his door came from one of the high school students wanting to buy some gum. I told him I only carried a couple of dollars and I asked him for the same amount in gas. At that moment a high school boy from the dance next door came over to us. He overheard our conversation and interrupted us by saying,

"Here is another $5 for gas. It should be enough to get you to Taree."

I thanked him, pumped the gas and jumped back into the car.

By now the contractions, about ten minutes apart when we started, seemed to shorten with each mile. We drove up to the emergency entrance of the hospital and Pavitra was admitted at once. I parked the car and went into the hospital carrying Sukita.

The first person I met must have received her social skills training by watching the movie, "One Flew Over the Cuckoo's Nest." Not only would she not let us into the delivery room, she also expressed her anger at us for having a baby and disturbing her coffee break.

"Wait outside!" she commanded.

By the time the doctor on call arrived, baby number two, delivered by the nurse on duty, made her début. Everything happened within twenty minutes of our appearance at the hospital. Kusum, the name we gave the baby girl, came two weeks early. An interesting fact about this daughter, who is now in her 30s, seems to be related to her birth. Kusum is always in a hurry. She did not wait for two more weeks before being born. She is still impatient and wants things done yesterday. She pursues life at a speed with which people cannot keep up. We barely kept up with her need to be born.

Pavitra stayed in the hospital until three o'clock in the afternoon. The doctor needed to be sure everything remained in order. We returned three days later to have the baby examined again. We returned to Elands after the final baby checkup and settled into the role of raising two children. Homesteading and adapting to a lifestyle of parenthood remained a challenge both Pavitra and I accepted.

This is the house that Jeff built.

While building our house several months before, a photographer arrived in our community. He traveled around Australia visiting different areas where people returned to the country and built their own houses. He said he would return when I finished our house and take pictures of it and other homes built in Elands.

Not long after Kusum arrived the photographer did return and took pictures of our home. The caption about my house in his book stated,

"He never put hammer to nail before."

This seemed to be a fair statement. The homesteading life expanded my building ability to a level of competence allowing me to become a carpenter for a few years upon my return to the states. The photo book containing the images of the homes became published after we left Australia. The local residence of Elands sent me a copy after I returned to the states. I still hold the time I spent in the homesteading lifestyle as a wonderful time of personal growth and expansion.

Within the next six months ,our life enabled us to expand our goatherd to six goats and start a small cheese making business. We either sold or bartered the cheese to our other community neighbors in exchange for eggs and other products they raised or grew. Goat cheese today is something found in the high-end grocery section. After having made goat cheese, I no longer think twice about the price. A lot of work goes into this product.

Pavitra's mother, Norma, arrived soon after the birth of Kusum. She also appeared after the birth of the first child, Sukita, when we lived in Agnus Banks. When 'mum' visited she went nuts over the girls. She dressed them up in little dresses and paraded them around the house. We were the first to provide her with grandchildren and she poured affection onto them in vast amounts. Norma traveled halfway around the world to see her Aussie family. She could afford the trip because she now lived in Spain with her oldest daughter. The English Pound went a long way in Spain during the 70's and 'mum' always saved for trips to see her three daughters and grandchildren.

During the time of family expanding and home building my father tried to visit as well. He could not come after Sukita's birth because of a heart attack. He possessed high cholesterol levels due to genetics. Dad also passed the genetic condition on to his children. In the 70's the only way to treat such a condition seemed to be diet and exercise.

My father took the diet and exercise regiment seriously and started to train for half marathons. He lost many pounds of weight and I hardly recognized him from some of the pictures he sent me. As a Taurus, the bull, he would charge into whatever he needed to do to in life. Lipitor and all those other heart medicines were not yet invented so surgery and a change in lifestyle seemed to be the only choice remaining.

Chapter 57
The Last Year in Australia

Soon after Kusum's birth all the other landowners who were absent for many months started to make their way back to the property. Ray became a bartender in Sydney and eventually a manager. Deborah wanted to return so Ray gave up the one job he seemed to be successful at. They both returned with some money in their pockets. Tim returned soon afterwards, with his wife and son. The returned owners all seemed to be ready to get things going again.

By now Pavitra and I developed a routine of growing and watering vegetables, milking goats and visiting friends in the area. We remained the only ones who completed a house. By now Ray hoped we would be gone. He turned out to be quite an adversary. He always needed some excuse as to why he did not get things done while doing the homestead lifestyle. We were his excuse.

I believe, even to this day, Ray thought living on the land would allow him a living lifestyle of being stoned, and drink whenever he felt like it. Back to the land people needed a work ethic of which Ray never possessed. He remained married to a spouse and surrounded by other enablers who continued to support his inability to grow. They made comments like,

"Poor Ray. He came from such a difficult childhood. We need to allow for his shortfalls and help him when we can."

I became a thorn in Ray's side. Every time we completed another big project our success seemed to drive him deeper into depression. He completed nothing to improve his living conditions and his family still lived in the house of Tim, the dwelling never finished. He told the others on the property Pavitra and I could not handle the 'back to the land' lifestyle. It turned out Ray became the person who could not cope with such a change. Married to a nagging partner trying to push him to do something didn't help. The pressure mounted and it became only a matter of time before he exploded again.

In 1978 change came to the community of Elands. Many new young couples arrived to build and live in the area. Others came only to stay for the summer's pot growing industry.

Much like the 70's in the states, the idea of free love started to filter over to Australia and through the Elands community. Couples began having flings with other members of the community and the idea of having sex with someone other than your spouse became a trend. Several married pairs joined in and within a year they were no longer together. The movie, Bob, Carol, Ted and Alice came out in the 70s and if you saw the movie you know how the wife swapping movie ended. Pavitra and I, plus a few other community members, did not get caught up in the idea of screwing your neighbor to find happiness.

A group of women arrived in the community and became a big part of the change in Elands. They appeared at all the social gatherings held on people's properties and, if the weather permitted, would soon be topless. The Australian version of the woman's liberation movement had arrived. I did not have a problem with these young ladies advertising their female endowments but bare breasts did make conversation with any of them a real distraction. Eye contact became difficult, to say the least and small talk like "what's your sign" never entered the discussion.

The rift between Ray and myself continued to deepen. He became a real distraction to anything the community attempted. A few of us bought a piece of land near the center of the town to start a tourist restaurant and store. Elands, the home of the highest free falling waterfall in Australia, attracted tourists but no facilities for these nature lovers could be found in town.

Group meetings with the community members were held in order to voice their needs and wants. Some members thought a co-op store instead of a restaurant would serve them better. When Ray arrived he would start smoking joints and passing around alcohol to others in the meetings. Within an hour the meetings would break up due to the substances interfering in the decision-making process. This disruptive behavior and attitude towards accomplishments convinced me he did not want anyone to become successful in any endeavors. Ray chose to sabotage everything around him and in the end, himself.

In November of 1978 Ray came up to our house with a message. He said the neighbors received a phone call reporting my father's death. I needed to call home. We owned no phone. Being completely off the grid meant communication to the outside world involved letters or carrier pigeons. I made a call from the farmhouse where we purchased one of our goats. I found out my father died in his sleep from a third heart attack. I knew at this moment the time to return home to the U.S. had finally arrived.

One of the circumstances helping me make the decision to return to the States came down to how I wanted my children to grow up and experience the world. I remained unconvinced Australia sat on the cutting edge of anything other then its' beauty. Racism and how they treated their native population disgusted me. The states seemed to have progressed much further with racial issues and as I write this book we have a black man as president. I am in communication with Greg Berry and he feels the Australian population will not elect a Black Prime Minister in his lifetime.

The other property members where we lived also made a decision I disagreed with. They wanted to get into the pot growing industry. I did not want to be a part of this direction. Always on the alert for drug enforcement agents and watching out for city youth coming up to steal the crop did not appeal to me as a lifestyle worth pursuing. If an arrest were made what do you do about your family and their well being? I also did not indulge in the use of the weed. The practice of meditation replaced the need to smoke and get high.

The last point helping to guide my decision centered on the time I spent away from home. For more than eight years I remained out of the States. Neither of my parents came to visit my family. We lived on the other side of the world and the call to return to my roots became stronger.

There remained much to do before we could leave Australia. Cars and tools needed to be sold. Passports and birth certificates required updating and tickets purchased for the flight back to America. The partners on the property did not want to co-operate by buying our property share. They would not allow us to sell our land portion to anyone else. The value of the land increased ten fold with a house, dam, an orchard of fruit trees and a garden. The goat house would remain empty because none of the partners wanted to milk goats and continue the cheese business. By now I knew we needed to leave and get away from these share owners. I accepted a price of $800 from Tim. The money covered our plane tickets back to San Francisco.

Qantas Airlines offering a travel deal we took advantage of. The cost for two adults and two small children round trip was $800. A one-way ticket priced out at $1200. The plan by Qantas existed for people living outside Australia to come and visit and then return home. We planned on going one way and not returning. I felt the guardian angel still at work making our trip possible and affordable.

I sold everything and set our return date for April. One of the women from the 'bare-breasted club' bought our Land Rover. She kept her top on during the transaction. I did not want to loose my shirt in the deal. Pumps and tools went to the weekly auction in Taree and everything else sold to neighbors supporting our decision. During this transition, we stayed with Gladney on his apple farm.

Our return to the states prompted Gladney to return to Pennsylvania to visit his family. His time spent away from the states also covered years. I later found out he took a job at a bookstore in the States which sold metaphysical books and stories about the occult. He told the owners he worked in a bookstore before so he got the job. After a few weeks, the owners started to question his experience and asked him when and where he worked in a bookstore. Gladney said it happened in England sometime during the eighteenth century. If you sell books pertaining to past lives and someone tells you he sold books in a previous life, what can you say in response? Gladney kept the job.

*****

My family and I stayed with another friend in Sydney right before our flight left for the States. We knew her before we moved to the country and she visited us several times in Agnus Banks. During our stay, my daughters kept discovering things they knew nothing about. The first item never seen before by the young girls was a switch on the wall. When the little knob went up the lights turned on. Pulled down and the lights went off. How could this be possible? Kerosene lamps started with a match was all they knew about lights while living in Elands.

The second discovery happened in another part of the house. The girls kept disappearing for periods of time and I did not know where they were. We finally found them in the WC or toilet room. They kept going into the WC and pulling the chain, which released the water in the tank above the toilet. They stood watching the water swirl around and down the hole in the bottom tank. Having never seen such a modern device as a flush toilet, they remained entertained for many minutes. Also, water in the toilet does spin the opposite way in Australia as it does in the Northern Hemisphere. The old fashioned out house is what those of us who homesteaded in Australia used. I knew then I made the right decision to get the girls back to civilization. If they wanted to live off the grid and go back to the country they needed to make the decision for themselves.

The flight was scheduled for 8 pm on April 29th and left right on time. We flew all night and arrived in

Hawaii in the morning. We went through the passport and customs office within sight of Honolulu and all the beautiful beaches. I have not returned to Hawaii since. We could have stayed a night but my brother was waiting for us in San Francisco.

The flight to San Francisco took as long as dinner and a movie. We landed at 7 pm on April 29th. We landed an hour before we took off in Australia. I think I will let the reader figure out what happened.

I left the States in September of 1970 and I returned in April of 1979. I returned to America married with two children. Eight years and seven months later I finally circled the globe. I believe I experienced more than the other guy who did it in eighty days. A book, as well as a movie, told his story. I have told many of these adventures to my friends for the past twenty-nine years. In the summer of 2009, I decided to write them all down.

Chapter 58
Looking Back

After reviewing this time in my life I sometimes wonder how my sense of the world might be different had I not left the States. The journey took place during all of the 70's. During this time the Vietnam War ended. Jimmy Carter, replaced after one term, went on to become one of the most accomplished men of our time. John Travolta became a star making a movie about Disco dancing. Stop signs all over California included the word disco painted beneath the word stop. Some family by the name of Brady seemed to be the hot item on the television. People prided themselves because they could repeat all the names of the children. I do not think I missed out on too much by not living in the States during the 70s.

The return to California and raising my family took on a normal lifestyle for us. I attempted to do carpentry for a few years but a building lull in the 80s brought the career to a halt. I went back to waiting on tables, a job I learned how to do on weekends in college. I finally started a job, which directed me towards a teaching career. I worked as a teaching aide in a group home school for problem high school students. I observed the teachers in the classroom and I knew I could also work in this profession.

By 1986 I earned a teaching credential while living in Redding, California. I moved to Santa Rosa fifty miles north of San Francisco to be near my daughters and continue to be a part of their life while growing up. They moved to the area of Sonoma County with their mother the year before. Pavitra and I separated in 1983. We seemed to take different directions in our lives. She still felt the isolated life of living in the country suited her best. I was done with the back to the land idea and sought a professional career with a population nearby.

Pavitra became a leader in the recycling business in her attempt to make an impact on the world. A company in Santa Rosa hired her based on the experience she showed working with a small recycling company in Redding.

In 1988 I hired on as a full-time teacher in a group home setting. I continued to work in schools for troubled students for the next twelve years. In 1992 I remarried and have been with my wife, Suzanne, for nineteen years. Somehow she still finds me somewhat interesting. She taught as an educator working with pre-school aged children. Suzanne helped me raise my daughters after they came to live with us full time starting in their Middle School years. Pavitra thought I possessed a better discipline ethic. The teenage years demanded a firm hand in the process of guiding strong-willed daughters.

By the year 2000 both Sukita and Kusum graduated from college. Sukita went to the University of Oregon and remains in this northwest living in Portland. She became a builder and pours earthen floors for people who want a natural look to their living quarters. Kusum went to my Alma Mater, UCSB and now lives in Oakland, California. She earned a Masters Degree in social work and is employed in the Oakland school district.

After Kusum graduated from college in 2000 Suzanne and I moved to Flagstaff, Arizona. We visited the Southwest before in 1998 including Zion and Bryce Canyon. Seeing the red rock and beauty of the Southwest for the first time inspired us to make the move. We decided to escape the high prices and crowded conditions of California.

I worked eight more years in the Flagstaff school system and retired from full time-teaching in 2008. Suzanne retired in June of 2010. She took a three-year break from 2002 to 2005 to become a minister of a New Thought church called Religious Science. We both were Religious Science Practitioners for many years but Suzanne wanted to take it to a higher level and she did. Meditation is still a big part of our routine in life and it is helping us get through the many transitions we face during retirement.

In 2011 Suzanne and I moved to a development in Baja near a town called San Felipe. I have written two more books since living here and am working on a fourth. Creative juices seem to flow in Mexico and we have done well adjusting to the cultural change.

Chapter 59
Where Are They Today

Since retiring I made contacts with friends, from college and high school. I also used Facebook to track down many of the travelers I came across during those nine years abroad. Here is the accumulation of my searches so far.

Steve Rewick, my travel partner in Europe, now lives in Bend, Oregon. He too has just retired. His return to the states directed him back to Santa Barbara again where he worked in the bar and restaurant business. The restaurant on the end of the pier where Steve poured drinks burnt down one evening. Steve came to work the next day to find his place of employment no longer in existence.

Bend Oregon became his next home where he continued in the food business by owning and running a restaurant by the name of Player's Grill. I visited him in the early 80s but did not tell him I was coming. I entered his restaurant with my two young daughters demanding service and doing so in a loud voice. As he approached he finally recognized me. Thirteen years passed since our last connection in Greece. We shared a good laugh and enjoyed a great meal.

The parents of Steve now live in Scottsdale, Arizona. When Steve and his wife Liz came out for a visit we would sit around and try to remember events from forty years before. I am sure our wives love listening to two old guys trying to put the stories of long ago into coherent sentences. Even to this day Steve said the eighteen months he spent in Europe were the most memorable of his youth.

Don, the person I traveled with in India and surfed the virgin waves, resurfaced (get it, re-surf-aced) on Facebook. I already had self-published the first edition of Living Beneath the Radar when I re-discovered my travel journal in storage. Don's real name, Parker Donaldson, appeared in the address section of the book. I entered Parker Donaldson under search and a picture of him came up. Forty years later and the resemblance still remained. A few messages and eventually an e-mail address and we reconnected.

Don lived in the countryside on the east coast for a few years. He returned to California at some time and now lived in the coastal town of Encinitas. The town is the same place where Paramhansa Yogananda started one of his many ashrams back in the 30s and 40s. Don and I visited the ashram of Sri Yukteshwarji in Puri, India in 1972. As you remember, Yukteshwarji introduced and trained Yogananda in the meditation of Kriya Yoga. I believe Parker never gave up his desire to be inducted into Kriya Yoga.

I visited Parker soon after I contacted him. Our family held a memorial service for Suzanne's mother, Alice, in the ocean community of Carlsbad, California, a few miles north of Encinitas. I drove to the apartment Don shared with his talented son. Both of them were artists and his high school aged son also played in a band. The desire to be near the ocean again may have contributed to his Encinitas move. On the outside porch, a surfboard lay against the wall. Surfing remained in his blood.

The visit remained short due to my commitments regarding the memorial service. Parker thanked me for the copy of the book I gave him. He later e- mailed me admitting he did not remember all the stories I wrote about in the book. I assured him they were all true and I wished him well.

Katie Henderson, Don's girlfriend in India, also appeared in the address section of my journal. Parker told me she lived in Hawaii and he gave me her phone number. After several attempts, she finally returned my call and we caught up with our lives. She now goes by the name of Dechen Groode and made Hawaii her home for thirty-five years. She and her husband, Jason, conduct spiritual retreats including Sufi Dancing, Zikr, and other meditation practices. She also sent me a short bio of her life since India.

Before going to India Katie worked for The Hollywood Reporter and Show Magazine. The stark contrast of India to the Hollywood lifestyle impacted her view of the world and guided her towards a more spiritual connection in life. Her new name, Dechen, means 'great bliss' and she received it from His Holiness The Karmapa. Besides the spiritual retreats she conducts in Hawaii, she practices Homeopathy and sells health products, primarily Natural Cellular Defense. She also returned to India on a pilgrimage to see her Homeopathy teacher in North India and Sai Baba in South India. India changed her way of being and guided her toward a spiritual lifestyle.

Paul, the Indian son of Mahendra who went to Holland, married his lawyer sweetheart. I heard the news while living in Australia. When Suzanne and I returned to Amsterdam in 2008 for a visit, I did not try to find out where Paul lived and how his life in the west played out. Too many years passed and I did not want to have anything to do with the family. I just needed to let them go, on many levels.

Kate and Robert, the couple who helped with our wedding in Bali, are still involved with meditation and spiritual practices. Katie went back to Massachusetts where she originally came from and became a founding member of the Vipassana Meditation Center in the state. In 1982 she married another person involved in meditation and both went on to become assistant teachers two years later. She now lives in rural Massachusetts, surrounded by a large garden and the wildlife found in the nearby woods.

Robert Pryor is also involved with spreading meditation and eastern practices in the west. Every year Robert takes a group of college students to Bodh Gaya in India as leader of the Antioch Buddhist Studies Program. He married twenty-two years ago to a woman named Dianeah Wanicek and together they also run Insight Travel, taking people on pilgrimage to India, Nepal, Bhutan, and Tibet. He happened to be in India at the time I contacted him through email. The second time he wrote back he was visiting the city of Puri, India. He informed me he had not seen the surfboard left behind by Don in 1972. If anyone who reads this book goes to Puri please visit the ashram and bring the surfboard back to California. It belongs in the Surfing Museum in San Diego or the Yogananda Ashram in Encinitas, California.

Ray and Deborah from the Australian back to the land adventure divorced a few years after we left Australia. I felt a sense of relief for Deborah. She finally left a relationship based on making excuses for a husband dependent upon drugs and alcohol. My daughter Sukita went back to Australia to visit the land where she was born. She connected with Deborah and her new husband along with Deborah's daughter Willow who lived not far from Taree. Little news of Ray existed.

A woman by the name of Helen Hannah lived in Elands the same time as we did and is writing a book about the area and the changes that have come about. She told me Ray lives in town but as a recluse. She wrote to him and wanted to see if he was interested in being included in her book. He never returned her letter. He ended up as the Elands person who hung around town doing odd jobs and surviving. I bet he remained on the dole. I do not have contact with any of the landowners other than Greg Berry.

Tim, who wanted to become the wise old wizard similar to Gandalf in the Lord of the Rings, is the only person remaining on the Doyles River property. He is surrounded by two hundred and fifty acres of gum trees and wildlife. His wife, Junko, lives in Sydney and visits Tim once a month. Greg says Tim looks a little frail. He is now in his 70s. Sukita, my daughter, took a few photos of the property and the buildings left behind. The house I built became an art studio where Tim and Junko weave cloth. Tim seems to have taken "Living Beneath the Radar" to a whole new level.

Greg Berry went back to school and earned a Ph.D. He now travels to different countries throughout Southeast Asia working with diet and other related subjects for the population in those regions. He still owns his share of the property in Elands. He also could not sell his house to anyone because of the land partners not allowing the transaction to happen. He since made some return visits in order to repair the house he built back in 1977.

Andy Colvin, the engineer who moved to Elands several years before Pavitra and myself, still lives in the area. I mentioned in the book he started a solar installation business. He installs panels for homes on and off the grid and the business seems to be doing well. Australia, like Arizona, is a perfect location for solar power due to the high count of sunny days. The surprising story Andy told me pertained to the fact he started a radio station in 1982 in Elands called 2BOB Radio. Besides doing a weekly morning show he also produces a Saturday spot called 'The Full Quid' and talks about environment issues. The reason I was surprised by the news pertained to the quiet manner of Andy. He seemed to be a man who chose his words carefully before he spoke and now he is on the radio. No time to think before you speak while on the air. The things one finds out about another after a long period of separation really 'blows my mind'. (60s phrase)

Gladney Oakley died in 1994. He must have been in his 70s because he was 50 when I lived in Elands. He returned to Australia from the states at some time and I heard he lived with his daughter in Sydney until his death. The apple farm in Elands must have been passed on to his children. It would have been a great retreat from the busy life of cities in Australia.

The author, Helen Hannah, told me a little about the community of Elands after we left. Her book has the working title, "A Peaceful Revolution- The Elands Alternative Community, 1970 -1995" and tells about the changes which came about in the 80s. According to Helen people with money began moving into the area, buying farms and land to remodel and build country estates. People with all the stress coming from making a lot of money need a place to retreat and unwind. She also said the marijuana industry reduced to an insignificant level due to the new money coming into the community. The old store, which served as a post office and gas station, still remains keeping the quaint country feeling of Elands alive.

Helen also told me the Bulga Community Cooperative is still in existence and owns the same property in town. The start of this organization became my last act along with Andy Colvin and a few others. I believe the business became a buyer of bulk food, which they in turn sold to the residents in smaller amounts. This service allowed residents to sell their extra produce from their gardens and reduce the trips down to the valley in order to purchase food staples.

Pavitra died in 2004 in her sleep. Her death came as a shock for Sukita and Kusum. They both remained close to their mother and the loss took a while for them to recover. Sukita used part of the money her mother left her and traveled around the world going from east to west. She did not want to take nine years like I did. New Zealand and Australia were her first stops. She visited Agnus Banks in Australia where she was born as well as Elands. Agnus Banks is now developed into large parcels for wealthy horse owners who replaced the old farmhouses with mansions and stables. She called me on the phone while standing near the property where she was born. In 1976 such a telephone call would not be possible.

Next year Suzanne and I plan to move to Baja, Mexico. We bought into an American development five years ago near the Mexican town of San Felipe. We visit every winter to experience sixty-degree weather in December. Living in a culture with a relaxed lifestyle is what we want in our retirement years. We will be only one hundred miles from the States so any emergency or visits to family can be easily accomplished.

Chapter 60
The World Has Changed

Retirement forces one to look at life in a different way. Work is such a large part of one's daily routine. When the job ends and you don't play golf then one needs something to fill the void. I always planned to write about the nine years of being away from the States and this experience. I have now done so and my wish is for the book to give the reader some insight into the world we live in and the people who make up the human race.

The disaster of 9/11 changed many American's acceptance for anything different. The cultures and religions of the culture found in America have been under attack from the fear-based population of today. I grew up with the historical knowledge that America took in refugees from all over the world. Here is the poem, written in 1883 by Emma Lazarus, found on the Statue of Liberty entitled The New Colossus.

"Not like the brazen giant of Greek fame
With conquering limbs astride from land to land;
Here at our sea-washed, sunset gates shall stand
A mighty woman with a torch, whose flame
Is the imprisoned lightning, and her name
Mother of Exiles. From her beacon-hand
Glows world-wide welcome; her mild eyes command
The air-bridged harbor that twin cities frame.
"Keep, ancient lands, your storied pomp!" cries she
With silent lips. "Give me your tired, your poor,
Your huddled masses yearning to breathe free,
The wretched refuse of your teeming shore.

**Send these, the homeless, tempest-tost to me,
I lift my lamp beside the golden door."**

I still believe in what America once stood for and hope we as a people can see the gift of living in a multi-cultural world not based on one religion or one language.

Looking back at the many things that happened amazes even me. Bringing Turkish puzzle rings to Greece and starting an exchange between two countries not friendly with each other falls under International Trade. Don and I were the first to surf in India. This adventure could be labeled Wide World of Sports.

Making a black-turbaned Afghan angry with the stinky infidel on the bus may have contributed (or not) to the start of the Taliban movement. I do not know what this story could be filed under. I wanted to contact the Levi Strauss Company and see if they could work the story into an advertisement showing the strength of their pants but now it is too late. The jeans are no longer made in San Francisco and the durability of the material is nowhere near what it used to be forty years ago. I still buy Levis today but the jeans are manufactured in Mexico, Egypt and othercotton growing countries around the world and do not maintain the high quality of denim from my youth in the 60s and 70s.

Seeing a Buddhist Nun just after she finished a six-year retreat, sealed in a cave, may be categorized under International Religious Tolerance. Finding the farm in Italy where I may have lived in a previous life could be a book found in the Occult section of Barnes and Noble. Seeing the energy force leave a dog, while in India, could place the book in the paranormal section of the same store.

Meditation and coming into contact with the Vipassana technique while in India remains a part of my daily routine. My sitting did go through a period of limited practice and I only meditated when my mind became overwhelmed. I now have a more routine approach in the mornings and acknowledge the benefits of this eastern practice as something every person in the west could use in their life no matter what church or religion they believe in. Meditation is not about believing this way or that way as an approach to God. It is a technique for the individual to help calm the mind, live a more peaceful life and to carry on what one is already doing in a more concentrated and productive manner.

I believe travel is the best education a person can obtain in their life. How else can one expand their view of the world without limitations? The news? Talk-show television? I don't think so. If you have a chance to travel, do it. There are still many safe places to go and experience the world. South America is one such region filled with ancient history. Remain open to the knowledge you will receive. They will be your adventures and yours alone.

Travel in the 70's was a lot easier than it is today because the earth was much different back then. All one needed was a passport and a desire to visit different cultures. Most of the Middle East was accessible and the route to India from Europe remained open until the late 70's. Those who passed through these areas of the globe got the chance to broaden their visions of other people along with their religions and customs. I made a comparison at the beginning of my journey in 1971 to the Lord of the Rings and the Hobbits of the Shire. Such adventures change one, be you a hobbit or a human and trying to share the adventures with others who did not make the journey is difficult. Frodo could no longer live in the Shire and left on a boat with Gandalf and the other Elves. I also have felt the isolation one has inside from experiencing the world and knowing truths about other cultures unknown to my countrymen.

Today the traveler cannot head east from Europe or visit all the countries found in South East Asia. Many areas of the world are closed off. Religious differences and extremists in many countries have caused the population of the U.S. to stay at home. Mexico, our neighbor to the south, is seen by many citizens as an unsafe place to visit due to the clashes on the border involving the drug trade. The fear of cultural differences seems to grip many who have never ventured from their homeland.

The educational degree of travel, earned by those who ventured out into the world during this window of opportunity, gave us the chance to meet, interact and understand the planet a little better. The human race speaks different languages but we all have the same needs. We worship in different churches, mosques, temples and Synagogues but we all believe in the same higher power. We follow separate customs and traditions and hopefully we are able to respect each other's differences.

The world is made up of a population of beings who are doing their best to survive and live together. No one language, religion or culture is right for everyone. The understanding and acceptance of this fact is the Ph.D. of understanding the world. We are all different and when this simple truth is learned and truly understood, we, as individuals, will be on the path of World Peace. This is what I learned and it can never be taken away from me. My views of the planet and America most certainly would have been different had I not left the states in 1970.

If by chance you come to Baja, Mexico and sit on the sand overlooking the Sea of Cortez, look and see if there is a guy in a beach chair reading a novel or magazine on his Kindle. Engage him in a conversation and ask him what he did during his life. He may tell you a story about his travels and how the world used to be forty years ago. You may wonder who he is and why you have never heard of him. I think the man sitting on the beach prefers it that way. He still enjoys "Living Beneath the Radar."

The Author on the beach in Baja reading his Kindle

Works Cited

Blair, Sheila S., Bloom, Jonathan M. "The Art and Architecture of Islam, 1250-1800"

   Yale University Press. 1994

Iran Chamber Society. "Cities of Iran". www.iranchamber.com/cities/mashhad.

October, 2009

Gray, Martin. "Amritsar, India". www.sacredsites.com/asia/india. 1983-2009

History of Goa. en.wikipedia.org/wiki/goa

Sri Aurobindo. en.wikipedia.org/wiki/Sri_Aurobindo

Paramhansa Yogananda. en.wikipedia.org/wiki/Pramhansa_Yogananda

Turkey. en.wikipedia.org/wiki/Turkey

Qutb Minar. en.wikipedia.org/wiki/Qutb_Minar#history

Jeffrey R Crimmel

ABOUT THE AUTHOR

Jeffrey Crimmel is an author who has eight published books on Amazon ranging from 'Travel, nonfiction' to 'Murder, mystery, fiction' focusing on the investigations of Robert Forrester.

After graduating from UC Santa Barbara in 1969 Mr. Crimmel decided to move to Europe and see the world. He had a degree in Geography and wanted to visit the planet in person and not observe it from a news reel. He traveled overland three times through Turkey, Iran, Afghanistan, and Pakistan to India. He eventually settled in Australia after continuing through SE Asia, and homesteaded in the woods of NSW. He returned to the California in 1979 with his wife and two daughters.

Mr. Crimmel earned a teaching credential and used his degree to teach in California and Arizona. He retired in 2008 and began writing down his adventures while traveling in the 70's. *Living Beneath the Radar* , *A Nine Year Journey Around the World,* is the book documenting that adventure.

A move to San Felipe and Baja California for three years created the time for Mr. Crimmel to write three more books. He is currently living in Ramona, CA with his wife, Suzanne, and two cats. Plans are to settle in Oregon in the near future and be near his daughter in Portland.

www.ingramcontent.com/pod-product-compliance
Lightning Source LLC
Chambersburg PA
CBHW051814090426
42736CB00011B/1477